STDs and HIV:
A GUIDE FOR TODAY'S YOUNG ADULTS

Student Manual

by
William L. Yarber

Sponsored by the
Association for the Advancement of Health Education
an association of the
American Alliance for Health, Physical Education,
Recreation and Dance

The American Alliance for Health, Physical Education, Recreation and Dance is an educational organization designed to support, encourage, and provide assistance to member groups and their personnel nationwide as they initiate, develop, and conduct programs in health, leisure, and movement-related activities. The Alliance seeks to:

- Encourage, guide, and support professional growth and development in health, leisure, and movement-related programs based on individual needs, interests, and capabilities.
- Communicate the importance of health, leisure, and movement-related activities as they contribute to human well-being.
- Encourage and facilitate research which will enrich health, leisure, and movement-related activities and to disseminate the findings to professionals and the public.
- Develop and evaluate standards and guidelines for personnel and programs in health, leisure, and movement-related activities.
- Coordinate and administer a planned program of professional, public, and government relations that will improve education in areas of health, leisure, and movement-related activities.
- To conduct other activities for the public benefit.

Special appreciation is given to Frankie G. Barnes and Annie Faye Prescott, Division of STD/HIV Prevention, Centers for Disease Control, Atlanta, GA, for their valued guidance and support during the preparation of this curriculum.

© 1993
American Alliance for Health, Physical Education,
Recreation and Dance
1900 Association Drive
Reston, Virginia 22091

ISBN: 0-88314-533-2

About the Cover

A dimensional illustration uses real objects to project a message. The objects represent important STD/HIV prevention strategies, myths about STD/HIV transmission, and aspects of young adult life. The messages of the cover components, as perceived by the illustrator (Joe LaMantia) and the author (William L. Yarber), are:

All objects are common items in young people's daily lives; so too are STD/HIV—the second most common types of communicable disease in the United States. **The yellow title letters** represent caution and a slowing down; young people should practice caution in the dating relationships and should "slow down" at any intimate experience to be sure they are making proper decisions about STD/HIV prevention.

The watch represents time—now is the time for young adults to learn about STD/HIV. **The cup and the doorknob** are to show that it is virtually impossible to get STD/HIV from such objects as cups, doorknobs, or toilet seats. **The rings** indicate that people's risky behavior determines whether they can contract STD/HIV, not whether they are married or unmarried, or in a heterosexual or homosexual relationship. **The children's clothing** in the word "and" symbolizes the more than 100,000 infants and children in the United States who die or suffer birth defects from STD/HIV each year. **The letter "H"** is a symbol of hope—a wish that people will become responsible for avoiding STD/HIV and that this problem can be ended soon.

The key in the letter "I" is to show that the individual, not the government or medicine, is the key component to controlling STD/HIV. **The combs**, of both females and males, represent the fact that both genders can contract STD/HIV, and both can work together to avoid STD/HIV. **The letter "V"** indicates that with continued efforts, we may someday be victorious over STD/HIV.

CONTENTS

Why Learn About STD/HIV?

Sexually transmitted diseases (STDs) are a serious health problem in our country. Once called venereal diseases (VD), STDs affect over 40 million persons a year in the USA. Young adults are especially affected by STDs. Every year, about 2.5 million teenagers — about one in every six — contract an STD. Every 13 seconds a teenager gets an STD in the USA.

STDs are passed during sexual contact with an infected person, by infected blood in injecting drug equipment, and from an infected mother to her child. Unless treated early, STDs lead to more serious health problems. STDs can cause sterility, nervous system damage, heart disease, arthritis, and harm to babies. One STD, AIDS, is a fatal disease.

Gonorrhea, syphilis, HIV infection and AIDS, genital herpes, chlamydia and genital warts are some of the important STDs. Nine important STDs are described in this book.

Even though STDs have always been a serious problem, many people have become particularly scared since the AIDS problem emerged. However, young adults should also worry about other STDs. They have a greater chance of contracting gonorrhea, chlamydia, and genital warts, for example, than HIV, the virus that causes AIDS.

You should learn about STDs because *your behaviors are the key to avoiding STDs*. Individual prevention is the most effective solution to controlling STDs. This book will help you learn how to avoid STDs. It will tell you:

- how STDs are and are not passed
- what to do to keep from getting an STD
- how to recognize STD symptoms
- where to get STD medical care and information
- how to get partners to treatment
- how one can help control STDs

Some of the terms used in this book may be confusing. Many terms are defined in the glossary. Use it to look up difficult terms. Before going further, one term should be defined. "STD/HIV" is frequently used to refer to STDs in general and HIV infection. This is done since the health behaviors of passing and avoiding most STDs and HIV are basically the same. Therefore, STD and HIV often should be discussed at the same time.

Now, go to the next page and read the objectives of the book.

Objectives

After completing this book, you should know and be able to discuss:

- the health problems caused by STD/HIV.
- how STD/HIV are and are not transmitted.
- ways to avoid STD/HIV.
- who can help you avoid STD/HIV.
- the major symptoms of STD/HIV.
- what to do if an STD/HIV infection is suspected.
- where you can get STD/HIV information, counseling, and testing.
- ways to get a sex or drug-using partner to a doctor.
- what can be done to help stop the spread of STD/HIV.

You should also be able to:

- recognize that STD/HIV are a serious problem among young adults.
- accept that risky sexual and injecting drug behavior can result in STD/HIV infection.
- feel responsible to practice STD/HIV prevention.
- accept the importance of others in helping you learn to avoid STD/HIV.
- feel responsible to get any sex or drug-using partners to treatment if you become exposed to or infected with STD/HIV.

- accept the responsibility of being a positive role model for STD/HIV prevention.
- be willing to provide accurate STD/HIV information and advice to others.
- desire to show support for persons with STD/HIV.

To help stop STD/HIV, you will:
- avoid sexual exposure to STD/HIV.
- not use injecting drugs or share needles.
- resist peer pressure to practice risky behavior.
- communicate STD/HIV concerns to friends and dates.
- avoid exposing others if an STD/HIV infection is diagnosed or suspected.
- seek prompt medical care if an STD/HIV infection is suspected.
- follow a physician's directions if treated for STD/HIV.
- get all sex and drug-using partners to medical care if you have STD/HIV.
- be supportive and helpful to persons infected with STD/HIV.
- serve as an accurate source of STD/HIV information and advice.
- serve as a positive role model to others.
- promote healthy behaviors among peers.
- seek the help of informed or qualified persons concerning STD/HIV issues.
- promote STD/HIV education, research, and health care.

SELF-TEST
Discovering What I Know - 1

Circle the letter T or F for each statement below to indicate True or False. Use another sheet if you cannot keep this book. You will not be graded on this test. Also, you are *not* required to answer these questions. But, it will show you how much you already know about STD/HIV. Use the Pronouncing Glossary on page 90 to look up words you may not know.

Answer Key: T = True
F = False

T F 1. There are several STDs other than HIV infection that young people should be concerned about.

T F 2. STD/HIV can be transmitted only by genital contact.

T F 3. The more sex partners a person has, the greater the chance of getting STD/HIV.

T F 4. Sexual abstinence is the most effective way to avoid STD/HIV.

T F 5. The use of a condom *eliminates* the chance of getting STD/HIV.

T F 6. The symptoms of most STDs are equally noticeable for females and males.

T F 7. A person who suspects that he or she has an STD/HIV infection should stop having sex and quickly get to a doctor for an STD/HIV check-up.

5

T F 8. Persons under the age of 18 are required to get permission from their parents to get STD/HIV treatment and counseling.

T F 9. Routine physical examinations usually include tests for STD/HIV.

T F 10. A person can get an STD again after being cured by having sexual contact with a parenter who is not cured.

T F 11. If an STD/HIV public health specialist contacts a partner of an STD/HIV-infected person, the specialist must tell the partner who gave his or her name.

T F 12. Persons with different partners should have regular check-ups even if they don't have STD/HIV symptoms.

ANSWERS: The correct answers are given below. The page number in this book where the answer is discussed is also provided.

1. T (p. 10)	5. F (p. 23)	9. F (p. 40)
2. F (p. 18)	6. F (p. 33)	10. T (p. 46)
3. T (p. 19)	7. T (p. 34)	11. F (p. 49)
4. T (p. 22)	8. F (p. 38)	12. T (p. 52)

SELF-TEST
Discovering What I Believe - 1

Circle the letter D or A for each statement below that is most like what you think. Use another sheet if you cannot keep this book. You will not be graded on this test. Also, you are *not* required to take this test. But, you might enjoy learning about some of your beliefs.

Answer Key: D = Disagree, A = Agree

D A 1. People are making too big a deal out of STD/HIV.

D A 2. People get infected with STD/HIV because they are being punished for their wrong actions.

D A 3. Practicing sexual abstinence to avoid STD/HIV is taking the STD/HIV problem too seriously.

D A 4. Using condoms to prevent STD/HIV is too much trouble.

D A 5. Persons infected with STD/HIV don't have any obligation to get their sex partners to a doctor.

D A 6. STD/HIV doctors and health care workers cannot be trusted.

D A 7. Anyone with an STD/HIV infection who gives the name of a sex partner to the doctor is a "squealer."

D A 8. People with an STD/HIV infection do not deserve help from others, because they get what they deserved.

7

D A 9. Students with an STD/HIV infection should not be permitted in school.

D A 10. It is best to stop being friends with someone who has STD/HIV.

D A 11. STD/HIV infection should be the concern of other cities and towns, but not mine.

D A 12. STD/HIV education in schools is a waste of time.

RESULTS: If you decided:

    D Your beliefs help control STD/HIV.

    A You lack an understanding about STD/HIV prevention.

STD/HIV FACT #1
The STD/HIV Problem

Did you know that...
- more than 25 diseases can be spread by sexual contact.
- many of the STD/HIV cases occur in young adults.
- STD/HIV can cause serious health problems and death.
- the number of AIDS cases in young adults is increasing.

A New Name for Venereal Disease

Sexually transmitted diseases,* or **STDs,** is a new term for **venereal diseases.** In the past, only a few **infections** were called venereal disease. Syphilis and gonorrhea were the most important ones in the United States. Recently, several more infections have been identified as diseases passed during sexual contact. Therefore, STDs is now the best term.

Some Important STDs

Scientists classify more than 25 diseases as STDs. Some STDs affect only a few people, and some do not cause serious health problems. Other STDs affect many people or cause severe body damage and death.

One STD, acquired immunodeficiency syndrome (**AIDS**), has become a very serious health problem. Many people have died from AIDS. Young adults who practice **risky behavior** can become infected with the human immunodeficiency virus (**HIV**), the cause of AIDS. Therefore, young adults should be concerned about AIDS. This book will discuss HIV infection and AIDS. It will also tell you how to avoid HIV.

---

* Words in bold print are defined in the Pronouncing Glossary on page 90. A guide on how to pronounce the most difficult words is also given.

However, HIV infection is not the only STD that should concern young adults. STDs such as chlamydial infections, genital herpes, and gonorrhea occur among young adults. They also can damage one's health. These and other STDs will be discussed here.

Nine important sexually transmitted diseases are listed in Table 1. You should know how to avoid them and how to get treated. You can learn more details from the Summary Charts of Important STDs that begin on page 80.

Table 1. Nine Important STD

Chlamydia Infections (klah-MID-ee-ul in-FECK-shuns)	A common cause of **pelvic inflammatory disease** and sterility in women and **urethritis** in men.
Genital Herpes (JEN-a-tul HERP-eez)	A disease caused by a **virus** that cannot be treated effectively.
Genital Warts (JEN-a-tul WORTS)	**Warts** found on or around the **genitals** or **rectum**. Often called venereal warts.
Gonorrhea (GON-oh-REE-uh)	A common cause of pelvic inflammatory disease and sterility in women and urethritis in men.
Hepatitis (hep-uh-TITE-us)	An infection of the liver, often not acquired sexually.
HIV Infection and AIDS Human Immuno- deficiency Virus	Infection with HIV can lead to AIDS. There is no cure or **vaccine** for HIV/AIDS.

(HYOO-men im-YOON-oh-de-FISH-un-see VY-rus)
Acquired Immunodeficiency Syndrome
(uh-CHOIR-d im-YOON-oh-de-FISH-un-see SIN-drome)

10

Pediculosis Pubis	Pubic lice or "crabs" found in the
(pa-DIK-you-LO-sis	pubic hair.
PUE-bus)	
Syphilis	Can cause serious body damage,
(SIF-i-liss)	but less common than other STDs.
Trichomoniasis	Common infection of the vagina.
(TRIK-uh-MOE-NYE-uh-SIS)	

Size of the Problem

Before this century, more people died from **communicable diseases** than from any other cause. Today, communicable diseases account for a small percentage of deaths in the United States. Their threat has been reduced through immunization, new treatment drugs, and improved nutrition and sanitation.

However, STD/HIV, which are communicable diseases, are still a major threat to health. They affect more than 40 million people in this country. Each year there are about 12 million new cases. The number of STD/HIV cases been increasing the past few years. STD/HIV are the second most common communicable disease (The common cold is first). Estimates of the present number of STD/HIV cases include:

  30 million genital herpes cases, with one-half million new cases each year
  12 million cases of genital warts
  4 million cases of chlamydial infections
  3 million cases of trichomoniasis
  1.5 million cases of HIV infection with over 200,000 persons diagnosed with AIDS
  750 thousand cases of gonorrhea
  125 thousand cases of syphilis

11

The first case of AIDS in the United States was reported in 1981. Since then, the number of cases has rapidly increased. Since AIDS is the end result of a long period of HIV infection, the number of AIDS cases is like the tip of a very large iceberg. The statistics above illustrate this: only about one-tenth of those believed infected with HIV have yet to develop AIDS. However, most **HIV-infected persons** are expected to eventually develop AIDS. A more detailed explanation of the difference between an HIV infection and AIDS is explained in STD/HIV FACT #3 on page 30.

Persons with STD/HIV

Anyone can acquire STD/HIV, regardless of age, sex, race, social status, or **sexual orientation.** Even infants can become infected before or during birth if the mother has STD/HIV. Who one is has nothing to do with your chance of becoming infected. For example, just being **heterosexual, homosexual,** or **bisexual,** does not cause STD/HIV. Engaging in certain risky behavior with an infected person exposes one to STD/HIV. Risky behavior is discussed in STD/HIV FACT #2 on page 18.

Most STD/HIV cases occur in persons in their mid-teens through their 40s. About two-thirds of STD cases other than AIDS are persons under age 25. A teenager in the United States gets a sexually transmitted disease every 13 seconds. STD/HIV cause serious damage to more teenagers than do all other communicable diseases combined.

STD/HIV has been **diagnosed** in many types of people. Children, teenagers, and adults — both females and males — have been infected. All races have been infected with STD/HIV. Every state in the United States has reported STD/HIV cases. STD/HIV cases are found everywhere, including small towns and rural areas, suburbs, and large cities.

AIDS cases are largely found among persons in their late 20s through the 40s. There are very few cases of AIDS in persons below age 20. Therefore, many young people feel that they do not need to worry about HIV infection. As you will learn later, an

12

HIV infection may have an **incubation period** of several years. This means that many persons in their 20s with AIDS became infected with HIV when they were teenagers. However, there is an increasing number of AIDS cases being diagnosed among teenagers.

Most AIDS cases in the United States have been found among (1) male homosexuals, or males who had sexual contact with other males, and (2) male bisexuals, or males who had sexual contact with both females and males. However, the percentage of the total AIDS cases from these groups has been decreasing. AIDS has also been diagnosed in **injecting drug** users, both heterosexual and homosexual. The percentage of AIDS cases resulting from injecting drug use is increasing among heterosexuals. Also, most AIDS cases in heterosexual men, women, and children have involved injecting drugs.

An increasing number of AIDS cases have occurred among heterosexuals from sexual contacts. In the United States, about 3 percent of males and 34 percent of females who have contracted HIV acquired the virus from the other sex. The World Health Organization (WHO) reports that about 75 percent of HIV-infected persons worldwide acquired HIV from heterosexual contact. Most of these cases are from Africa, Asia, and Latin America.

Others became infected with HIV through **blood transfusions** or blood products. The vast majority of these infections occurred before 1985, the year screening of blood donations began.

AIDS cases have also been found in most countries of the world. WHO has indicated that over 150 countries have reported at least one AIDS case. WHO estimates that 11 to 12 million adults worldwide are infected with HIV.

Damage from STD/HIV

The list of problems caused by STD/HIV seems almost endless. Without medical attention, some STDs can lead to permanent body damage. For example, blindness, cancer, heart disease,

13

sterility and even death can occur. Women and infants suffer more serious health damage than men from all STDs. However, many more males have died from AIDS.

Several billion dollars are spent yearly for STD/HIV tests, treatment, health care, research, and education. Time is lost from school and work. Lives are shortened. Time spent for medicine and research on STD/HIV could be used for other health problems.

The outcome of having AIDS is very severe. Persons with AIDS can become very ill, with much pain and suffering. They may also have to spend long periods of time in the hospital. Persons with AIDS usually develop or acquire diseases that can lead to death. About three-fourths of persons having AIDS in the United States have died. The total is over 140,000 deaths. More than 100 people die of AIDS each day in the United States. Most lived less than two years after they developed AIDS. No one has completely recovered from AIDS.

Untreated STDs in women can cause pelvic inflammatory disease (PID). Each year several million women in the United States suffer from PID. The germs that cause gonorrhea and chlamydial infections are the most common cause of PID. They damage the reproductive system, leading to **ectopic pregnancy**, miscarriage, and infertility. Even though PID can be cured, there may be repeated pain in the pelvic area for many years.

Untreated syphilis in adults can cause heart damage, blindness, insanity, and death. Infants born with syphilis can suffer brain damage, blindness, deformity, and death.

Genital herpes cannot be cured. Once the virus enters the body, it remains for life. The virus produces painful, itching sores on or around the genitals that last several weeks. In some people, these sores recur several times during a year. Babies born of women infected with herpes are at risk of permanent health problems and death.

Cancer of the **cervix** is known to occur more often in women with genital herpes and genital warts. However, it is uncertain if these viruses cause this common form of cancer.

14

Why the Problem?

There are many reasons why STD/HIV is such a large problem. For example, the biology of many STDs, and peoples' risky health behaviors and poor living conditions contribute to the STD/HIV problem.

In some ways, STDs are more difficult for medical providers to deal with than many other communicable diseases. STDs caused by a virus such as HIV infection and genital herpes, cannot be cured. Some STD germs have become **resistant** to treatment drugs. Only one sexually transmitted disease, hepatitis B, has a vaccine. Further, some STDs do not have early **symptoms** of infection.

Certain health behaviors lead to more STD/HIV. For example, some people practice risky sexual behaviors or have sexual contact with high-risk persons, such as **prostitutes.** Some may have many sex partners. There is a high rate of **sexual intercourse** among young people. And some people fail to use **condoms** during risky situations.

Having an STD may cause some people to feel guilty or ashamed. Therefore, they may delay or avoid treatment. Some people, especially those infected with HIV, may avoid medical care because they fear discrimination. Finally, some infected people fail to inform a sex partner about the need for medical care.

Injecting drug use has lead to high numbers of persons being infected with HIV. STD/HIV has also been spread because some people have sex in exchange for drugs. That is, they receive drugs or money from sex partners so they can support their drug addiction.

There has been an increase of STD/HIV among disadvantaged people. Inner-city, poor, minority populations have been particularly affected. Among these groups, teenage females have the highest STD rates. Inner-city living conditions make it difficult to practice a healthful lifestyle. For example, many cannot afford private health care. Hence, the treatment of an STD is often delayed. This increases the chance that the STD may be passed since the person may not know about the infection.

Persons who contract STD/HIV need the help and support of others. Efforts to blame or shame STD/HIV patients are likely to do more harm than good.

— — — — — — — —

Check-up: (Write answers here only if you can keep this book.)

1. STD/HIV are the second most common type of communicable disease in the United States.   TRUE   FALSE

2. HIV infection is the only STD that should concern young adults.   TRUE   FALSE

3. STD/HIV cause more serious damage to more teenagers than do all other communicable diseases combined.

           TRUE   FALSE

4. When considering all STDs, which group of persons suffer the most serious body damage?_____

5. What are some major reasons why STD/HIV are such a serious problem? _____

_____

Answers to Check-up:

1.   TRUE. Some health experts suggest that STD/HIV are more common than all other communicable diseases besides the common cold. STD/HIV affect over 40 million people in this country. Each year there are about 12 million new cases.

2.   FALSE. Other STDs such as chlamydia infections, genital herpes, and gonorrhea occur frequently among young adults. They also can produce lasting health damage.

3. TRUE. Most STD/HIV cases are persons in their mid-teens through their 40s. About two-thirds of STD cases other than AIDS are persons under 25.
4. Women and infants suffer more serious health damage from STDs than do men. But, more males have died from AIDS.
5. There are many reasons why STD/HIV are such a serious health problem. Major reasons include the biology of STDs, people's risky health behaviors, and socio-economic conditions.

What Do You Think? (Answer these questions in your mind. Don't write them anywhere.)

1. Should a person feel guilty and ashamed if he or she gets STD/HIV? Why?
2. Do people become infected with STD/HIV because they are being punished for their wrong actions?
3. Is it right to discriminate against people with STD/HIV?

Life Situation #1: (Try solving this problem before reading the answer.)

Some young people in your town practice behaviors that put them at risk for STD/HIV. They don't seem too worried about STD/HIV. They think that STD/HIV are not a big problem for people of their age. These young people also believe that STD/HIV are not a problem in their town, even if other places have a high STD/HIV rate.

QUESTIONS: Are these people right in what they believe about STD/HIV? If you had a chance, what could you say to help them understand the STD/HIV problem? (See page 59 for the answers.)

STD/HIV FACT #2
Avoiding STD/HIV

Did you know that...

- STD/HIV are passed (1) during sexual contact, (2) by infected blood in injecting drug equipment, and (3) from an infected mother to her child.
- sexual abstinence, mutual monogamy, condom use, and avoiding injecting drug use are the best ways of avoiding STD/HIV.
- learning to communicate is necessary to avoid STD/ HIV.

STD/HIV Organisms

STD/HIV are caused by organisms that can be passed from person to person. These organisms include **bacteria, protozoans,** viruses, and very small insects such as the pubic louse. They are usually found in **semen, vaginal fluids**, and blood.

Transmission of STD/HIV

Specific ways STD/HIV are **transmitted** are described below. A person can get STD/HIV many times. That is, a person does not develop an **immunity** to STD/HIV after being infected and treated. Also, scientists believe having one STD may put a person at risk for getting another STD. For example, a person with an STD who engages in risky behavior with an HIV-infected person may have a greater chance of becoming infected with HIV. A person can have more than one STD at a time.

    Sexual Activity. Sexual intercourse with an infected person is the most common way STD/HIV are transmitted. They can be passed during **vaginal intercourse** or **anal intercourse**. **Oral-genital** or **oral-anal** sex may also be ways STD/HIV are transmitted. That is, STD/HIV are spread when infected semen, vaginal fluids, or blood enters the partner's mouth, **penis, vagina**, or rectum. However, a few STDs such as genital herpes or genital warts can be spread by direct contact with infected skin.

People have worried that they can get STD/HIV from deep kissing. This way of transmitting STDs is rare. For example, HIV has been found in saliva, but in very small amounts. No cases have been reported of persons getting HIV from kissing, even open mouth, deep "French" kissing.

STD/HIV can be passed from one sex to the other, as well as from male to male and from female to female. Many cases of HIV have been passed during sex between two males. But, few cases of female to female transmission of HIV have been found. STD/HIV are not as serious a problem among **lesbians** as among heterosexual women. However, lesbians still should be alert about STD/HIV, especially if they share **injecting drug equipment**. Remember, people's behavior—not who they are—exposed them to STD/HIV.

Sexual Lifestyle. Persons who do not have sexual contact with anyone are not likely to get STD/HIV. Persons with one partner rarely acquire STD/HIV, unless the partner is using injecting drugs or has other sex partners. People with many sex partners have the greatest chances of getting STD/HIV. They increase the risk with each new partner they have. The chances of infection are high if any of these persons have several sex partners, or have other risk factors that are described later.

Blood Transmission. Blood-to-blood contact between an infected person and someone else is one way some STDs, mainly HIV, can be passed. Actually, blood transmission is the second most common way HIV is passed. This method of transmission is now almost entirely limited to persons injecting **illicit drugs.** The sharing of injecting drug equipment, such as needles and **syringes,** allows the exchange of blood.

Donated blood has been tested for the HIV **antibody** since 1985. The supply of donated blood is safer than ever before. Persons at risk for having STD/HIV are requested not to donate blood. Persons who donate semen, body tissues, and organs are tested for HIV antibodies. Therefore, it is very unlikely that a person could become infected with HIV from a blood transfusion. To be absolutely safe, some people who know they will have surgery donate their own blood a few weeks before surgery. It is then stored in a blood bank and used during surgery if necessary. A common myth is that a person can get HIV from donating blood. This is not true. A different needle is used for each donor.

HIV can be transmitted by ear piercing or tattooing if the equipment is not sterilized properly.

Mother to Child. A pregnant woman who has STD/HIV can pass the disease to her baby during pregnancy or at birth. Estimates are that each year more than 100,000 infants die or suffer birth defects from STD/HIV they got from their mothers. About one percent of AIDS cases in the United States occur in children, mostly who acquired HIV from their mothers. A child has about a 50 percent chance of being born with HIV if the mother is infected. Babies born with HIV usually die within two years. HIV may be passed to a child during breast-feeding.

STDs Without Sex. You may have heard that STD/HIV can be contracted from objects like door knobs, toilet seats, drinking glasses or from **casual contact**. It is virtually impossible to get STD/HIV in this manner. Certainly there have been no reported cases of HIV contracted from objects like door knobs or toilet seats. Light and air destroy the STD/HIV organisms very quickly.

Most STDs, like gonorrhea, syphilis, and genital herpes, are very unlikely to be caught from an object. Pediculosis pubis ("crabs") can be acquired from contaminated clothing and bedsheets. HIV and hepatitis can be acquired from contaminated needles.

The ways HIV is transmitted has been misunderstood. These myths have caused many people to have an unreasonable fear of AIDS. For example, they may be afraid of HIV-infected persons and refuse to be near them. However, HIV is not like other communicable diseases, such as the flu, cold, or measles.

These diseases can be spread through sneezing, coughing, or being around an infected person. HIV cannot be spread that way. HIV cannot be spread by casual, social, or family contact. No cases have been found where HIV infection was transmitted by just being near infected persons. Even family members living in the same household with an infected person have not gotten HIV.

People can work with others, use public toilets, telephones, and swimming pools, eat at restaurants, and attend public events without the fear of getting HIV. Children with HIV infection pose no risk for other students in schools.

HIV is **not** spread by:
- sneezing, coughing, or spitting
- hugging, holding hands, or kissing
- sweat, tears, urine, or bowel movements
- dishes, eating utensils, or food
- mosquitos, bed bugs, lice, or other insects
- using toilets, sinks, bathtubs, swimming pools, or telephones
- using someone else's comb or make-up
- being near an HIV-infected person in school or other places
- donating blood

Remember, HIV is transmitted in only three ways: (1) sexual contact with an infected person, (2) sharing injecting drug equipment with an infected person, and (3) an infected mother to her child during pregnancy, childbirth, or breast-feeding.

Prevention of STD

Since STD/HIV are transmitted by certain behaviors, we know exactly how to keep from getting them. The preventive actions are actually easy to do. People sometimes do not practice them because of a lack of skills or motivation. You can avoid or reduce the risk of STD/HIV by doing the things listed below.

Sexual Abstinence. The best way of not getting STD/ HIV is to not have sex. This is done by practicing **sexual abstinence**, meaning not having any type of intercourse or oral sex with anyone. Even though sexual feelings are natural, sexual abstinence in young adults is also a normal and healthy choice. Many young people have decided to delay intercourse.

Young people who are abstinent usually have fewer problems than those who get sexually involved too early. Certainly those who are abstinent do not need to worry about pregnancy. Early sexual activity has serious physical and mental health risks. People can be close or have a special relationship without having intercourse. Some express intimacy by touching and massaging.

Many religious groups in our society believe that sex should be postponed until marriage. Other factors, such as maturity, age, and personal and family **values** should also be considered when deciding whether to have sex.

Mutual Monogamy. Uninfected partners who practice **mutual monogamy** in a long-term, steady relationship or marriage will not get STD/HIV through sexual contact. This means that both partners are faithful and did not have STD/HIV when they started having sex. These couples can continue to avoid STD/ HIV if they are monogamous and neither partner shares injecting drug equipment.

It is not always possible to know if a partner is monogamous or is infected with STD/HIV. This is one reason why it is wise to wait for sex until a person can form a long-term, mutually monogamous relationship with an uninfected partner.

Reducing Risk During Sexual Intercourse. In some situations, persons should avoid exposure to certain fluids from a partner's body. This should be done if sexual contact occurs outside a monogamous relationship. This is also true if one is not sure the partner has STD/HIV or shares injecting drug equipment. Basically, a person should not allow blood, semen, or vaginal fluids to touch his or her genitals, mouth, or anus. One of the best ways to prevent these fluids from entering the body is by proper

22

use of the latex condom. The latex condom is much better protection against STD/HIV than the natural membrane (sheepskin) condom. The latex condom will have the word "latex" on the package.

Proper use includes putting the latex condom on the penis before any sexual activity begins, not just before intercourse. An empty space should be left at the tip of the condom to collect semen. It should be kept on during any time the penis touches the partner. One should not allow the condom to slip off the penis when it is removed after intercourse. Also, a condom should never be reused.

The condom can greatly reduce the chance of getting STD/HIV and pregnancy. But, a condom is not 100% effective. It is possible for a condom to leak, break, or slip off. Using birth control foam, cream, or jelly, along with a latex condom, may provide more protection. Other birth control methods, such as birth control pills, do not protect the user against STD/HIV.

Douching, washing, or urinating after sex have been suggested as possible ways to reduce chances of infection. Effectiveness for these methods has not been proven. Therefore, do not rely on them to avoid STD/HIV.

Careful Partner Selection. A person should avoid sex with persons who might be a high risk for having STD/HIV. For example, does the person have many sex partners or use injecting drugs? This method is not always reliable. It is usually impossible to determine who has an STD/HIV by just looking, or by the person's reputation. Also, the person may not be honest about their sexual partners or drug use. Therefore, even if sex partners do not know each other well, they should exchange names and phone numbers. Then, each person can reach the other if an STD/HIV infection or another problem occurs.

Certainly a person should use a condom if the partner is not well known. Even then, the chances of infection increase with a partner at risk.

It would be helpful to know if a partner is at risk, or has had partners at risk. But, of course, it is not always possible to know if a person is at increased risk. Having sex with any of the following increases your chance of HIV infection and many other STDs:

- persons who test positive for HIV
- persons with medical evidence of HIV infection
- males who have had sexual intercourse with other males
- persons who have used injecting drugs
- persons who have had several sex partners
- persons who have any sexually transmitted disease
- female and male prostitutes
- persons who received blood-clotting products and blood transfusions before 1985
- sex partners of infected persons or persons at increased risk

Avoid Multiple Partners. Avoiding many sex partners helps keep one from getting STD/HIV. The more sex partners a person has, the greater the chance of getting STD/HIV.

Avoid Injecting Drugs. Another sure way to avoid HIV is not to inject drugs. Persons using injecting drugs certainly should not share the needles and syringes. Not only can drugs harm one's health, but they might also alter one's judgement. That is, a person drinking alcohol, smoking marijuana, or using cocaine or crack may not be able to think clearly or make wise health decisions. Their chance of engaging in risky behaviors is greater.

The most responsible health decision is not to use any harmful drugs. Anyone using drugs illegally should see a physician or counselor to try to stop the drug use.

Vaccines. There is a vaccine for only one STD, hepatitis B. Scientists are working especially hard now to develop a vaccine to prevent infection with HIV. However, it appears that it will take many years for an HIV vaccine to be developed.

Protecting Babies. Nearly all STDs can be transmitted from a mother to her baby before or during birth. In most cases, proper medical treatment can protect the baby from permanent damage. HIV-infected mothers should not breast-feed their babies. Since HIV infection cannot be cured, women who have HIV should avoid pregnancy.

Any woman thinking about becoming pregnant should know if their partner has STD/HIV. Women who are or who plan to become pregnant should insist that their partner use a condom if he may have practiced risky sexual behavior or used injecting drugs. A woman who gets pregnant should have a check-up for STD/HIV. If a woman has STD/HIV and becomes pregnant, she should tell her doctor.

Other Prevention Methods. One way to reduce, but not eliminate, risk is to insist that partners be tested for STD/HIV before starting to have sex with them. This method has become more important because of the HIV problem. Most of the people infected with HIV do not know it. Old test results are not reliable, especially if the person has since engaged in risky behaviors. And, some persons may not be honest about test results.

One could look for **signs** of STD/HIV, such as sores, rashes, or pus from genitals before sexual contact begins. Of course, this method is also not reliable since one can have STD/HIV without having symptoms. One should look for symptoms on the partner, as well as on oneself. Certainly the couple should avoid sex if either has STD/HIV symptoms.

Persons infected with STD/HIV should avoid exposing others. They should practice sexual abstinence or **risk reduction**. HIV-infected persons should not use injecting drugs nor share the injecting equipment. Likewise, HIV-infected persons should not donate blood, bone, organs, semen, and tissues. Lastly, they should also advise their sex or injecting drug partners to go to a physician.

Communicating Prevention to Others

One important skill needed to avoid STD/HIV is the ability to effectively communicate with others, especially persons who might be sex partners. Persons need to learn how best to communicate their thoughts, feelings, values, needs, and standards of behavior. Research has shown that good communicators are less likely to do things against their values or beliefs. It is very important that a dating couple be able to talk openly with each other.

One should feel free to discuss concerns about STD/HIV with any possible sex partner. Stating that you care about the health and well-being of both of you can be a way of starting the discussion. One should not have sex with a person who will not talk about such issues.

To be a good communicator, you should be clear about your beliefs and values. Then you should stand by them. You might want to plan what to say ahead of time. You also could talk to your friends, a counselor, teacher, or religious leader to learn how to improve your ability to communicate with others about values.

Improving Communication. Being a good communicator takes practice and work. Here are some suggestions on how to improve communication:

- pick a good time and place to talk
- be clear about your beliefs and values
- decide what to say at the beginning
- take the initiative to start the talk
- discuss why talking is important
- use "I" messages
- use positive nonverbal messages, such as eye contact
- listen carefully
- provide feedback
- respect the other person's views and values
- be specific about your values and needs
- try to negotiate conflicts

26

Resisting Negative Peer Pressure. Each of us faces peer pressure. Sometimes, the pressure is negative. For example, someone may try to force you to use drugs. Usually, making a wise decision and sticking to it when someone is pressuring you is difficult.

Everyone needs to learn to resist negative peer pressure. There are things you can do now to improve this skill. For example:
- learn your family's and your own values
- practice resisting negative peer pressure and sticking to your values
- avoid persons who might pressure you to practice risky behavior
- learn to identify risky situations

When actually pressured to practice a risky behavior, try some of these ideas:
- state your decision; repeat if necessary
- state why you refuse to take the risk
- be firm when talking
- take action, which may be leaving the scene
- suggest an alternative activity

Persons often fear that resisting pressure from a dating partner or friend will result in loss of the friendship. Certainly, this may occur. But, a true friend would respect your decision and remain your friend. One thing that you can do is to suggest a mutual activity that is not risky. For example, as an alternative, you could invite the person to go to a movie with you. Then, suggest that the person call you later if he or she wants to go. This shows that you are trying to keep the friendship.

Help for Avoiding STD/HIV

Choosing behaviors that avoid STD/HIV can sometimes be difficult. This is especially true if a person feels like he or she is alone in making the decision. It helps if others provide encouragement and support.

Do not hesitate to talk with people you trust about decisions related to STD/HIV. Seek the advice of people you respect. Persons who might be helpful are:
- parents or guardians
- religious leaders
- teachers, school nurses, counselors, or youth leaders
- other trusted adults
- friends who are good role models

Also, talk with your parents, religious leader, or another trusted adult about sex and growing up. They can help you understand your sexuality and develop a **sexual code of behavior**.

— — — — — — — — —

Checkup: (Write answers here only if you can keep this book.)
1. Sexual intercourse with an infected person is the most common way STD/HIV are transmitted.   TRUE FALSE
2. Deep kissing is a frequent way STD/HIV are transmitted.

TRUE FALSE
3. What are the three ways STD/HIV are transmitted?

_____

4. What is the surest way to prevent STD/HIV?

_____

5. What is the most effective preventive measure for persons with different partners? _____

Answers to Check-up:

1. TRUE. STD/HIV can be passed during vaginal intercourse or anal intercourse. Oral-genital or oral-anal sex may also be ways STD/HIV are transmitted.
2. FALSE. The transmission of STD/HIV by kissing is rare.

28

Lately, there has been much concern about the transmission of HIV by kissing. There have not been any reported cases of HIV being transmitted this way.

3. STD/HIV are transmitted in only three ways: (1) sexual contact with an infected person, (2) sharing injecting drug equipment with an infected person, and (3) an infected mother to her child during pregnancy, childbirth, or breast-feeding.

4. The surest way of not getting STD/HIV is to avoid sexual contact with infected persons.

5. The latex condom should be used anytime the penis touches the partner.

What Do You Think? (Answer the questions in your mind. Don't write them anywhere.)

1. Are most young people willing to practice sexual abstinence or mutual monogamy just to prevent STD/HIV?

2. Why don't more people use the condom when having sex? What could be done to make the condom more appealing?

3. Why is it difficult for some dating couples to talk about STD/HIV prevention? What can be done to help couples communicate better?

Life Situation #2: (Try solving this problem before reading the answer.)

Jennifer is 18 years old and has a younger sister, Kelly, who is 15. Jennifer and Kelly are very close and often talk to each other about personal things. Kelly knows that Jennifer learned about STD/HIV in school and asks her how a person can keep from getting STD/HIV.

QUESTION: If you were Jennifer, what would you tell Kelly about avoiding STD/HIV? (See page 59 for the answer.)

29

STD/HIV FACT #3
Recognizing an STD/HIV Infection

Did you know that...
- the major symptoms of STDs are genital discharge, abdominal pain, painful urination, skin changes, genital itching, and flu-like symptoms.
- the symptoms of HIV infection include tiredness, swollen lymph glands, fever, loss of appetite, loss of weight, diarrhea, and night sweats.
- the symptoms of HIV infection may not appear until a few months to ten years or more after HIV was acquired.
- a person who suspects an STD/HIV infection should: (1) stop having sex; (2) stop using injecting drugs; (3) promptly go to a doctor or clinic; and (4) get sex partners to a doctor or clinic.

HIV Infection and AIDS: A Special Case

The terms HIV and AIDS confuse some people and are often used improperly. There is a difference between an HIV infection and having AIDS.

Being Infected with HIV. Being HIV-infected means that a person has acquired HIV. That is, the virus is in that person's body. The person is considered infected even if AIDS does not appear. This person can pass HIV to others.

HIV destroys certain cells in the body that help the **immune system** fight off diseases. Therefore, the HIV-infected person may get serious illnesses more easily. HIV-infected people can acquire certain diseases that a person with a healthy immune system usually does not get. These diseases are called **opportunistic diseases**. Often such diseases are severe and lead to death. A certain severe lung infection and a rare skin cancer are examples of two common opportunistic diseases.

30

Some HIV-infected persons do not know they have HIV until symptoms of opportunistic diseases appear. Even then, they cannot be sure the symptoms are due to AIDS until they are tested for the presence of HIV.

Having AIDS. In general, an HIV-infected person must have one of the opportunistic diseases to be classified as having AIDS. Other serious health conditions resulting from having HIV may also indicate AIDS. Having AIDS means that HIV has caused so much damage that certain diseases have become established in the body. These diseases--not HIV itself--are what usually makes the person with AIDS so ill. Not all persons with HIV infection have developed AIDS, although most probably will as time progresses.

Being Aware of Your Own Body

Anyone practicing risky behavior as described in STD/HIV FACT #2 on page 18 should be alert to the symptoms of STD/HIV. This is especially true for persons having sex with different partners, or whose partners are at risk for STD/HIV. Any unusual or unexplained changes in one's health may indicate STD/HIV. Of course, the changes could be caused by other diseases. Changes in the genitals, especially, may be caused by an STD. However, symptoms of some STDs can appear anywhere on the body.

There are many sexually transmitted diseases. Many of them cause symptoms that are similar to other diseases. The symptoms of STD/HIV can be complex and confusing. Doctors often cannot tell if a person has STD/HIV by just looking. So, a person should not try to diagnose his or her own condition. That's the doctor's job. The important thing is for the person to recognize when there might be an STD/HIV infection and to see a doctor promptly. The sooner a doctor finds out which, if any, STD is present, the sooner treatment can begin for the person and his or her partners. Then, there is less chance of damage from an STD, or that it will be passed on to someone else.

31

Important STD/HIV Symptoms

To help avoid STD/HIV, a person should know what symptoms to look for in oneself and others. The major symptoms for most STDs are listed below. The specific symptoms of HIV infection are presented separately below. A person might have an STD if any of these symptoms are present: (The Summary Charts of Important STDs that begin on page 80 list the symptoms for nine important STDs.)

Genital Discharge. For men, pus may come from the penis. This may indicate gonorrhea, a chlamydial infection, or other STDs. The discharge may be white, yellow, clear and watery, or thick. Women may have an unusual discharge or smell from the vagina. Since the discharge is often slight and inside the vagina, it may not be noticed. It may not seem much different than the normal moisture in a woman's vagina. Further, STDs may cause bleeding from the vagina other than the regular menstrual blood flow.

Abdominal Pain. Women may have **abdominal** or lower pelvic area pain from an STD, which may indicate pelvic inflammatory disease. Also, there might be pain deep inside the vagina during sex.

Painful Urination. A burning feeling during urination, or frequent urination, may be a symptom of an STD, particularly for males.

Skin Changes. These symptoms include blisters, bumps, rashes, sores, or warts. Sores or blisters may be a symptom of syphilis or genital herpes. They may not be painful. Most often, they appear on or near the genitals. But, they could also appear on the mouth or rectum. A rash may indicate syphilis, and a person can acquire pink or reddish warts on or near the genitals. Further, there may be swelling around the sex organs.

Genital Itching. Itching on the genital areas, or other body parts, may be a symptom of pediculosis pubis (crabs). In females, itching may be caused by infections of the vagina.

Flu-like Symptoms. The person may have fever, chills, and aches.

Symptoms of HIV Infection. The first symptoms of HIV infection are similar to common minor illnesses, like a cold or the flu. Symptoms of persons infected with HIV can include tiredness, swollen lymph glands, fever, loss of appetite, loss of weight, diarrhea, and night sweats. The symptoms may mean that the person has HIV. Of course, other illnesses show these symptoms. HIV-infected persons may have these symptoms some or all of the time. Usually, the symptoms get worse and occur more often as time progresses.

The incubation period for an HIV infection ranges from a few months to ten years or more. However, a person can transmit HIV soon after he or she becomes infected, even before symptoms appear. It seems that HIV can be passed to others throughout the infected person's life.

Having an STD/HIV Without Symptoms

Some STDs do not have any symptoms until the disease is well-advanced. Often the symptoms disappear, and then come back again, as described above for HIV-infected persons. Actually, a person can look and feel healthy and still be infected with STD/HIV. For some STDs, the early symptoms disappear without treatment. Infections inside the mouth or anus are hard to notice. Most STDs can still be passed on to someone even though the symptoms are not noticed, are absent, or disappear.

Males are likely to notice STD symptoms earlier than females. One reason is that the male genitals can be seen more easily. Most women who have an STD do not know they are infected. For example, up to 80 percent of women with gonorrhea do not notice symptoms. Therefore, women are at a greater risk of attaining serious problems from STDs. About 20 percent of men with gonorrhea do not have symptoms.

What to Do After Suspecting STD/HIV Symptoms

Stop Having Sex. A person should stop having sex once STD/HIV are suspected. This prevents the disease from being transmitted to any partner not already infected.

Stop Using Injecting Drugs. The sharing of injecting drug equipment may pass HIV to others. Further, continued use of injecting drugs may weaken the body's ability to combat an STD/HIV infection.

Go to a Doctor or Clinic. Go to an STD clinic, an HIV/AIDS clinic, or to a doctor right away if symptoms of STD/HIV are detected. Put aside feelings of guilt or shame. The important concern is to get medical treatment promptly. Do not use home remedies, products bought in the mail, or drugs from friends. Only qualified medical people can give the correct care. Persons suspecting STD/HIV shouldn't gamble that it might be something else or that it will go away. They should get a complete STD/HIV check-up from a doctor. Places that diagnose and treat STD/HIV are discussed in STD/HIV FACT #4 on page 38.

Get Partner to Treatment. Persons who think they have STD/HIV should also try to get their sex partner(s) to a doctor or clinic right away. Since the first warning that a woman has an STD is often when her male partner is infected, female partners especially should be advised. Partners who have no symptoms of an STD should still see a doctor. Suggestions on how to get a partner to a doctor are given in STD/HIV FACT #5 on page 47.

— — — — — — — — —

Check-up: (Write answers here only if you can keep this book.)

1. What determines when an HIV-infected person has AIDS?
_____

2. What are six major symptoms of STDs? _____
_____
_____

34

3. A person has STD/HIV only when the symptoms are present.

TRUE   FALSE

4. What four things should be done by a person who suspects an STD/HIV infection? _____

_____

Answers to Check-up:

1. In general, an HIV-infected person must have an opportunistic disease before being classified as having AIDS.
2. The major symptoms of STDs are: (1) genital discharge; (2) abdominal pain; (3) painful urination; (4) skin changes; (5) genital itching; and (6) flu-like symptoms.
3. FALSE. The symptoms of STD/HIV are sometimes absent or not easily noticed. However, the person may still have the disease, and it can be passed to someone else. More males than females have early symptoms of STD.
4. A person suspecting an STD/HIV infection should: (1) stop having sex;(2) stop using injecting drugs; (3) go to an STD clinic, HIV/AIDS clinic, or doctor quickly; and (4) get the sex partner to a doctor or clinic.

What Do You Think? (Answer these questions in your mind. Don't write them anywhere.)

1. Would most young people be alert to the most common symptoms of STD/HIV?
2. How would you feel if you gave an STD/HIV infection to someone? How could you deal with your feelings?
3. Would most young adults, after being diagnosed as having STD/HIV, notify a sex partner that he/she might have STD/HIV?

35

Life Situation #3: (Try solving this problem before reading the answer.)

James and Thomasina are having sexual intercourse. Sometimes, James has sex with someone else. A few days ago, James noticed some painful blister-like sores on his penis and feels like he has the flu. He hopes that the symptoms will go away without seeing a doctor. The blisters are too painful for James to continue having sex with Thomasina and the other partner. Thomasina hasn't mentioned any problems with her genitals, so James doesn't tell her about the sores. Then, in a couple of weeks, James's sores disappear. He now thinks he is all right, decides not to go to a doctor, and starts having sex again.

QUESTION: Did James do any correct things? What should he have done in this situation? What information about STDs did James not know? (See page 60 for the answers.)

36

STD/HIV FACT #4
Seeking Treatment

Did you know that...
- minors can get STD/HIV medical care in every state without their parents' permission.
- public STD and HIV/AIDS clinics, private doctors, family planning clinics, and hospitals are major places to get STD/HIV treatment.
- STD/HIV treatment will be more successful if the patient follows the doctor's directions exactly.
- there is no cure or vaccine for HIV infection or AIDS.

A person who thinks he or she might have STD/HIV should go to a doctor right away. The sooner one goes, the less likely the person will become seriously ill or give the STD to someone else. Remember, people who think they might have STD/HIV should not try to diagnose or treat themselves.

Confidential Treatment for Minors

Some young people can talk with their parents about having STD/HIV. However, some cannot and wouldn't want their parents to find out if they have an STD. These people are sometimes afraid to go to a doctor or health clinic. They're scared that their parents will be told. Keeping the information from parents may not be a problem if the STD is treatable and there are no serious problems. However, if a young person's parents knew the child had a very serious STD, such as an HIV infection, they might be very helpful. Hopefully, the child would receive parental support and understanding.

37

In every state, minors can be checked and treated for STD/ HIV without their parents' permission. The law applies to persons 12 years old and over in some states, and 14 years and over in other states. Call your health department or an STD or HIV/ AIDS clinic to find out about the law in your state. Also, the medical records of all STD/HIV patients are **confidential.**

Finding Medical Help

Sources of STD/HIV Care. STD/HIV medical care is usually easy to find. Your teacher or another adult can help find local sources for STD/HIV help. In most places, there are several choices of where to go. Most large communities have a public STD clinic run by the health department. Also, many cities have special HIV/AIDS counseling and testing clinics, also operated by the health department. These clinics usually do a very good job diagnosing STD/HIV. They are also very skilled in treating the STD or helping the person find medical care. Further, they make the person feel as comfortable as possible during the visit. A family doctor or another private doctor can provide medical help. Lastly, many family planning clinics and hospitals can test and treat people for STD/HIV.

Using the Local Telephone Book. Calling the local health department is one of the best ways of finding STD/HIV medical care in your town. The health department is usually listed in the telephone book yellow pages under county or city government offices. Sometimes, the health department is listed in the white pages under "health", or in the blue pages of government listings. The person calling should ask where to get STD/HIV help. A person can also call the local information operator to find the health department telephone number.

Some cities and states now have an AIDS telephone hotline. The hotline could suggest a clinic for both STD and HIV/AIDS. Also, a person can call a local crisis telephone hotline for information on local STD/HIV care.

National Hotlines. There are two national hotlines that can provide information about any STD. They can also suggest a place to get medical care for STD/HIV. The National STD Hotline (1-800-227-8922) is open for calls from 8:00 a.m. to 11:00 p.m., Eastern time, Monday through Friday. A taped message is given on weekends and holidays. The National AIDS hotline (1-800-342-AIDS) is open for calls 24 hours a day, 7 days a week. Spanish-language callers can dial 1-800-344-SIDA. Hearing-impaired callers needing TTY/TTD service can dial 1-800-AIDS-TTY.

A call is free and will not be charged to the phone bill as a long-distance phone call. The telephone operators do not ask the caller's name or make the person feel uncomfortable. They are trained to provide accurate information. They give callers good advice on what to do and where to go.

Remembering Sources of Help. There is a place on the inside back cover of this book where you can write the source for STD/HIV information and health care in your town. Then, if anyone ever needs to know where to go for help, it can be found quickly. Write in the book only if you can keep it. If you cannot, ask your teacher for a copy of the page.

Money Problems. If money is a problem, a person should still seek proper treatment. Most public STD and HIV/AIDS clinics or birth control clinics will treat a person for free. Some may charge a small fee. No one needs to delay seeking help because of a lack of money.

The Medical Visit

Counseling About Testing. Most people do not need to worry about getting STD/HIV, since they have not practiced risky behavior. However, persons at risk or suspecting infection should contact a physician or health care counselor. These professionals will help one decide if STD/HIV tests are needed.

Many local health departments provide confidential counseling and testing to all persons, including teenagers. Some also have

anonymous testing for HIV infection. If your health department does not have counseling and testing, it can still help people get these services.

Helping the Doctor. An STD/HIV examination is not the same as a routine check-up. Special tests are done to find out if a person has STD/HIV. The examination will not be done unless the person asks for it.

Facts that are known only to a patient can help a doctor decide which tests and treatment should be given. A patient should inform the doctor why STD/HIV are suspected. This might include any symptoms that the patient has noticed or any knowledge that a sex partner has STD/HIV. A patient should also tell the doctor what parts of the body have been exposed and when the contact took place.

Detecting an STD/HIV Infection. Examination and testing for STD/HIV is easy. People examined for STD/HIV do not need to be tested for all of the possible diseases. In most cases, two or three tests need to be done. None of the tests are very painful, nor do they take much time.

First, the doctor will examine the patient. This is done to see if there are any signs that the patient did not notice. Then the doctor will probably take a small sample of blood from the patient's arm. Next, fluid, if present, is taken from the patient's genitals or other exposed areas with a cotton-tipped swab.

The HIV-antibody test, a blood test, can help determine if a person has HIV. The test measures antibodies to HIV in the blood. The test is very accurate, but not 100 percent perfect. The doctor may also look for signs of HIV infection, such as an opportunistic disease.

Four different HIV-antibody test results are possible. A positive test means that the person has been infected with HIV. This does not mean that the person will develop AIDS, although it is likely. Certainly, the person can transmit HIV and should practice HIV prevention. On rare occasions, the test results may be positive when there are no HIV antibodies present. This is called false positive. Further test results usually show the true

40

negative finding.

A negative test result means that the person does not have HIV. There are no antibodies found in the blood. However, the test may have been taken before antibodies develop. It takes between 6 to 12 weeks for HIV antibodies to develop. Hence, the test should be taken at least 12 weeks after high-risk behavior. Also, on rare occasions a person may test negative when antibodies are present. This is called false negative.

It is a very bad idea for someone to donate blood to find out if they are infected with HIV. HIV counseling and testing through a health department or a doctor is best.

Sometimes a doctor can tell right away if a person has an STD/HIV infection. At other times, the doctor must wait several days before test results can be known. Treatment may begin on the first visit in either case. This is more likely when the patient is known to have been exposed or when certain symptoms are present.

STD/HIV Treatment. STDs are not all treated in the same way. The type of treatment given depends on many factors. The doctor must decide which drug is best for each case. Sometimes, the doctor injects medicine. In other cases, the doctor may treat an STD with pills or creams. The patient should always find out what is to be done or not done to make sure that the treatment will work. He or she should take the drugs or medicines exactly the way a doctor prescribes and should not be share them with others. A person must continue to take the pills until they are all gone, even if the person feels better or the symptoms go away. If the pills cause the person to feel ill, the person should call the doctor or clinic.

Most STDs can be cured in a short time. However, there are no drugs yet that can cure an HIV infection, AIDS, and genital herpes. Some new drugs slow the growth of HIV and improve the person's health. But, the person still has an HIV infection and can die of AIDS. Scientists are trying to create new treatments for HIV infection and AIDS, but progress is slow. A cure or vaccine for HIV/AIDS is not expected soon. Herpes can be treated to

41

reduce the frequency and length of the outbreak of blisters, although the disease cannot be cured.

A person diagnosed with an STD should not have sex until he or she is cured. Persons with an HIV infection should not have sex or should carefully practice risk reduction, such as condom use.

A person treated for an STD may be asked to return for follow-up tests and treatment. Even when the symptoms have disappeared, these tests are important. They are the best way to determine if the disease has been cured or not. Remember that a person can have STD/HIV and not have any symptoms.

Sex and Drug-use Partner Referral. If a person has an STD/HIV infection, the doctor, a nurse, or someone with special training may talk to the patient about sex and injecting drug partners. The partners may need treatment also. Ways in which partners can be informed are discussed later in this book in STD/HIV FACT #5 on page 46.

Support for Persons with STD/HIV. As you can imagine, discovering that one has an STD can be very upsetting and frightening. This is especially true for persons who become infected with any incurable STD, like HIV infection or genital herpes.

HIV-infected persons wonder if they will ever develop AIDS. They are concerned about exposing others to HIV. Persons diagnosed as having AIDS face even more severe problems. They will probably become very ill and die from an opportunistic disease. They also may be mistreated and have severe financial problems. Many persons with AIDS feel isolated and emotionally depressed.

Persons having the genital herpes virus also worry about exposing others to the virus. Women with genital herpes who want children are concerned about passing the virus to the baby.

Persons infected with an STD, particularly HIV and genital herpes, need the support of family and friends. They should realize that there are many others facing the same problem. Many health departments provide counseling or can lead persons

42

to others who can give support. Anyone infected with HIV should receive professional counseling.

Many persons infected with HIV or genital herpes have found help from support groups. Many towns have formed HIV/AIDS support groups for both the patient and the family. The American Social Health Association (ASHA) has a special program for genital herpes, called the Herpes Resource Center This center provides information and a newsletter. ASHA also helps organize local herpes support groups. Over 40 states have a local herpes support chapter. To get more information about herpes or local chapters, contact the National Herpes Hotline at 919-361-8488 during weekdays between 9:00 a.m. and 7:00 p.m. EST.

— — — — — — — — —

Check-up: (Write answers here only if you can keep this book.)

1. Young persons can receive STD/HIV counseling and medical care without the permission of parents.   TRUE   FALSE

2. Where can a person get STD/HIV medical care? _____

_____

3. What is one of the best ways of finding STD/HIV medical care in one's own town? _____

_____

4. What are some important things a person should do after being diagnosed as having STD/HIV? _____

_____

Answers to Check-up:

1. TRUE. In every state, minors can be tested and treated for STD/HIV without their parents' consent. The law applies to persons 12 years old and over in some states, and 14 years old and over in others. Call an STD or HIV/AIDS

clinic, or the local health department if you want to find out the age for your state. In some cases, however, if a young person's parents know that the person has a very serious STD, they can be helpful. Hopefully, the parents will provide support and understanding.

2. Places that can give STD/HIV treatment include public STD or HIV/AIDS clinics operated by the health department, private doctors, family planning clinics, and hospitals.

3. Calling the local health department is one of the best ways of finding STD/HIV medical care in your own town.

4. Anyone diagnosed as having STD/HIV should (1) follow the doctor's directions during treatment, (2) stop having sex until cured or practice prevention if the STD cannot be cured, (3) be sure that partners have been, or will be, checked for STD/HIV, and (4) return for follow-up tests or treatment.

What do You Think? (Answer these questions in your mind. Don't write them anywhere.)

1. Could most teenagers, if they got an STD/HIV infection, discuss the illness with their parents? Could you? Why? If you were a parent, would you want your child to tell you?

2. How would most teenagers feel about going to a doctor or clinic for an STD/HIV test? Would they be afraid or would they feel comfortable?

3. What would be your most important concern if you just learned that you have an STD?

4. If you got an STD, would you want to talk to someone about it? If so, whom?

Life Situation #4 (Try solving this problem before reading the answer.)

Maria, age 17, discovers from a sex partner that she might have an STD. This makes her feel ashamed and guilty. She knows that she should go to a doctor. But, she's afraid to see her family doctor, fearing that her parents will be told. She doesn't know where else to go for tests since she doesn't have much money of her own.

QUESTIONS: How could Maria find out where to go for STD/HIV tests? What information does she need to know about teenagers getting STD/HIV treatment and receiving care without much money? What could you say about STD/HIV to decrease Maria's feelings of guilt and shame? (See page 60 for the answers.)

STD/HIV FACT #5
Getting Partners to Treatment

Did you know that...
- the major reasons for getting sex and injecting drug-use partners to a doctor are to: (1) prevent serious illness in the partner, (2) prevent reinfection, and; (3) help control the spread of STD/HIV.
- one of the best ways to be sure a partner gets treatment is to take him or her to the doctor or clinic on the first visit.
- STD/HIV public health specialists can contact partners if the patient does not want to, or cannot.

Persons who acquire STD/HIV and get it treated have done the right thing. However, they have met only part of their responsibility. Helping sex and injecting drug-use partners get to a doctor is also important. Partners must be notified quickly.

Why Get Partners to a Doctor?

Prevent Serious Illness in Partner. Helping a current or previous partner to treatment might spare him or her from getting very sick from an STD. A lot of pain and suffering can be prevented. Remember from STD/HIV FACT #3 on page 33 that many persons—particularly women—don't have any early, noticeable symptoms of most STD infections. Symptoms may not appear until the disease has become advanced. At that stage, serious health problems may have developed. Also, the partners may have passed the disease to others without knowing they were infected. A person's warning may be the partner's first clue that they might have STD/HIV. Therefore, it is important to get sex and injecting drug-use partners to treatment quickly.

Prevent Reinfection. A person can get reinfected with a curable STD by a partner who is not treated. This can happen if

46

sexual contact resumes before an infected partner is cured. An STD can be like a dangerous ping-pong game, going back and forth between two people. The persons should not begin to have sex again until both have been cured.

Help Control the Spread of STD/HIV. Getting a partner to treatment will help control the spread of STD/HIV. Not only will the partner be treated, but that person can encourage any of his or her other sex and injecting drug-use partners to be treated. Hopefully, once a partner learns about his or her infection the person will be sure not to pass the infection to others. For example, knowing if one has HIV is especially important. Many HIV-infected persons have transmitted HIV to others when they did not know about their infection. HIV has been spread unknowingly to many people.

Ways of Getting Partners to Treatment

Taking Partner to the Clinic. One of the best things a person can do is to take the sex or injecting drug-use partner to the doctor or clinic during the first visit. Doing this helps get a partner, and the partner's partners, treated sooner. If a person waits until after being diagnosed, the person can still offer to take the partner to the clinic. Having someone to go with might make the partner feel more comfortable.

Certainly a person suspecting an STD/HIV infection must tell the partner why the person should go to a doctor with him or her. When talking with the partner try to be honest, don't blame anyone, remain calm and positive, and be supportive. These general suggestions apply whether a person suspects an STD/HIV infection or already knows of an infection.

Inform Partner Directly. If a person can't take a partner to the clinic or doesn't want to, the partner still needs to be informed about a possible infection. The infected person can do this face-to-face or over the telephone. Some people would rather tell their partners themselves. Others want someone else, like an STD/HIV **public health specialist,** to inform them. Most people

47

probably know best how their partner would want to find out.

Be sure to stress the importance of the partner seeing a doctor right away. Talking to a partner directly would also be a good chance to share any emotions that one might have about getting STD/HIV or giving it to someone else. Talking about it can help a person deal with these feelings.

Telling the partner that he or she might have an STD may be uncomfortable. This might be particularly true if the STD is a serious one, such as an HIV infection. A counselor at the STD/HIV clinic or a doctor can help a person decide how to inform the partner. But, telling the partner may not be as bad as one thinks. If a person doesn't know how, here's an example of what one person said to his partner:

> "Selina, I want to talk with you. It's not easy telling you this, but I've got gonorrhea. I'm sorry, but that means you might have it too. I've been to a doctor and got it taken care of. I'll be all right. But, the doctor says you need to be checked and treated very soon. Even if you don't have any symptoms you still might have it and get real sick if you are not treated. You need to see a doctor before that happens. You can go to the clinic where I went. They won't tell anybody that you were there, not even your parents. It's no hassle. I care about what happens to you. I want to help you. Let me take you to the clinic. Selina, please let's go right away!"

An STD/HIV Public Health Specialist Can Help. A doctor or STD/HIV public health specialist can help you notify partners. Even though the doctor doesn't actually do the contacting, he or she knows how to get in touch with a public health specialist. Informing partners is very important for their health and for preventing the spread of STD/HIV. A person isn't being disloyal by giving names to a public health specialist. Caring for the partner's health is a sign of loyalty and maturity. It does the partners a great favor by helping get them to medical treatment.

Talking with the STD/HIV public health specialist may be helpful even if a person doesn't know the name of a partner. (Remember the suggestion in STD/HIV FACT #2, page 23, that everyone should get the name and phone number of all sex partners.) Public health specialists can often locate people even without having their names.

Public health specialists talk with partners privately and inform them that they might have been exposed to STD/HIV. They also help get partners to a doctor or clinic. The public health specialists don't scold people or pass judgement on them. All of the information is kept secret. Also the identity of the person who gave his or her name is not mentioned to the partner.

— — — — — — — — —

Check-up: (Write answers here only if you can keep this book.)

1. What are the three main reasons why it is important to get a sex or injecting drug-use partner to a doctor? _____

_____

2. People can get reinfected with an STD if they resume sex after treatment and the partner has not been treated. TRUE FALSE

3. What is the best way to make sure that a sex partner gets treatment? _____

4. STD/HIV public health specialists will tell a partner where his/her name was obtained.   TRUE FALSE

Answers to Check-up:

1. Preventing serious illness in the partner, preventing reinfection in one's self, and helping control the spread of STD/HIV are the major reasons for getting a partner to treatment.
2. TRUE. A person can become reinfected if sexual activity resumes before an infected partner is also cured.

3. One of the best ways a person can be sure that the partner gets STD/HIV treatment is by taking him or her to the doctor on the first visit.
4. FALSE. Information about the source of his/her name is kept secret. An STD/HIV public health specialist will never mention a person's name to the partner.

What Do You Think? (Answer these questions in your mind. Don't write them anywhere.)

1. Would most young people feel comfortable taking a sex or injecting drug-using partner with them to an STD/HIV clinic or doctor? Why?
2. How would you feel about telling a partner he/she might have STD/HIV?
3. How would you want to find out that someone had exposed you to STD/HIV? Would most teenagers want to be told by a sex partner or a public health specialist?
4. Is giving a sex partner's name to the STD/HIV public health specialist "squealing"?

Life Situation #5 (Try solving this problem before reading the answer.)

Kevin learns from his doctor that he has an HIV infection. But, he doesn't like the idea of telling his partner, Pat. He says that he just doesn't know what to say. He finally decides not to talk with Pat since, according to him, the symptoms will develop soon anyway. Pat then will know that something is wrong and will go to a doctor, says Kevin.

QUESTION. Was Kevin correct in not talking to Pat? Why? What are some things that Kevin could say to Pat? In what other ways could Pat have been informed? (See page 61 for the answers.)

50

STD/HIV FACT #6
Stopping the Spread of STD/HIV

Did you know that...
- being responsible for your health and the health of any sex or injecting drug-use partner is the best way to stop the spread of STD/HIV.
- informed persons are better able to avoid getting and passing on STD/HIV.
- you can serve as a responsible role model and accurate source of STD/HIV information and advice.

Individual Efforts: The Key to STD/HIV Control

STD/HIV have become very common. Millions of persons suffer both physical and emotional damage from the diseases. Young adults, females, and babies suffer the most. Such organizations as the Centers for Disease Control of the U.S. Public Health Service, the American Social Health Association, the American Venereal Disease Association, and local health departments are conducting programs to control some of these diseases. The work of these groups is valuable. However, the best way to fight STD/HIV is by the efforts of individual persons. STD/HIV can be controlled — and there are ways you can help.

Being Responsible for Your Health
and the Health of Others

One of the best ways you can help control STD/HIV is by taking responsibility for your own health and well-being. This also means being responsible for the health of any sex and injecting drug-use partner. You can do this in several ways.

    1. **Avoid STD/HIV.** Of course, if everyone tried to avoid getting STD/HIV, fewer people would suffer damage from the

diseases. People who do not get STD/HIV avoid their health problems and can never pass them on to sex and injecting drug-use partners or infants. The surest way to avoid STD/HIV is not to have sexual intercourse or share injecting drug equipment. If a person chooses to have intercourse, it should be only within a long-term, mutually monogamous relationship. Any sex partner should be chosen with care. For example, persons with STD/HIV symptoms or who have many partners should be avoided. Other preventive measures, such as the condom, should also be used.

2. **Pay Close Attention to Your Own Body.** If a person has sexual intercourse or oral sex with others, it is important to be alert to any changes in the genitals or other parts of the body. This is especially true if the person has more than one partner. Genital discharge, abdominal pain, painful urination, skin changes, genital itching and flu-like symptoms are the major symptoms of STD infection. The first symptoms of HIV infection include tiredness, swollen lymph glands, fever, loss of appetite, loss of weight, diarrhea, and night sweats. Remember, the symptoms of STD/HIV infection are often hidden, absent, or unnoticed.

3. **Seek Medical Care.** Anyone having sexual intercourse or sharing injecting drug equipment should seek prompt medical care if any of the STD/HIV symptoms appear. For HIV infection, persons having the symptoms for more than two weeks should see a physician. He or she should also go to a doctor or STDHIV clinic if the symptoms aren't present, but an STD/HIV infection is suspected. Persons having sex with different partners should have regular STD/HIV check-ups. These check-ups are especially important for females since they often do not have early symptoms.

4. **Avoid Passing on STD/HIV.** Once a person knows or even suspects he or she has STD/HIV, being responsible to others means not passing on the infection. This is done by not having sexual intercourse or sharing injecting drug equipment until the disease is cured or until the person finds out that he or she is not infected. Of course, if the person has an incurable STD, such as an HIV infection, the person should practice abstinence

or risk-reduction. Also, a pregnant woman with STD/HIV should get proper medical care to avoid passing the infection to her baby.

5. **Get Partners to Treatment.** The final step is for everyone with STD/HIV to accept responsibility for getting sex and injecting drug-use partners to medical care.

Keeping Informed About STD/HIV

Being informed about STD/HIV means that the person knows (1) how STD/HIV are spread; (2) how to keep from getting STD/HIV; (3) how to recognize an STD/HIV infection; (4) when and where to go for medical care and other help; and (5) how to get sex and injecting drug-use partners to doctors or clinics. Informed persons are better able to avoid getting and passing on STD/HIV. They are also more likely to get any suspected STD treated before serious health problems develop.

You have taken the first step to becoming informed about STD/HIV by reading this book. You can also stay informed by calling the National STD Hotline or the National AIDS Hotline that were previously mentioned (see inside back cover for the telephone number). Other sources that can either provide information or help you get it are:
- parent or guardian
- religious leader
- local health department
- physician
- health teacher or school nurse

Remember, there's a space on the form (inside back cover) where you can write the place in your community that has STD/HIV information. Further, most libraries and bookstores have books about STD/HIV. And, the American Social Health Association will send pamphlets. (Single copies are free. There is a charge for quantities.) Contact: American Social Health Association, P.O. Box 13827, Research Triangle Park, North Carolina 27709 (phone: 919-361-8400 or 1-800-227-8922).

Promoting STD/HIV Prevention Efforts

1. Serve as a Responsible Role Model. As you learn about STD/HIV, you can help others avoid STD/HIV infection. One of the most important things you can do is to serve as a positive role model for your peers. If you practice STD/HIV prevention, you are setting a healthy example for your peers and those younger than you. Your responsible health behaviors, along with promoting prevention with your friends, may influence others to practice prevention. Support those who practice prevention. Also, being a responsible role model means that you should not pressure others to practice risky behavior.

2. Promote Healthy Peer Norms. Some young adults engage in behaviors that expose them to STD/HIV infection. Sometimes, these behaviors are considered the standards or "norms" of behavior of all young adults. Young adults practice risky behaviors for several reasons. For example, some may believe that many young people engage in risky behaviors. Peers may pressure them to behave a certain way. Further, some may believe that certain risky behaviors are the only way to have fun.

As a person who knows important STD/HIV facts, try to influence your peers norms to be more healthy. You can, for example, inform your peers that not all young people engage in risky behaviors. State that avoiding risky behaviors is both "normal" and "wise." You can teach others how to deal with peer pressure. Also, you can help create and promote ways of having fun that do not expose persons to STD/HIV infection.

3. Serve as an Accurate Information Source. You can be a good information source for your friends. Tell them that you have learned about STD/HIV and are willing to talk about it. There are many false ideas about STD/HIV. You can correct such myths by sharing what you have learned. Inform your peers where they can get more information or help. Finally, you can share this book with your friends, parents, and others.

4. Support STD/HIV Control Efforts. Besides practicing STD/HIV prevention, there are several things you can do to help stop the spread of STD/HIV. For example, you can support STD/HIV education in your school or town. Be willing to serve on advisory committees or to testify at hearings about the need for STD/HIV education. Help create an STD/HIV resource center of accurate information in your town or school. The center could contain articles, research reports, pamphlets, and books. Call your state or local health department or the National STD Hotline or the National AIDS Hotline for ideas about materials.

The STD/HIV Summary Sheet, found on page 98 can be distributed. Seek permission to reprint it in your school newspaper or post it on a school bulletin board. You could volunteer for STD/HIV control efforts in other ways. For example, you could assist persons with AIDS and their families. Some may need transportation to treatment or help in home care. Call the local health department or STD/HIV clinic to see what you can do. Volunteers also can organize an educational program or direct group efforts to influence guidelines and mandates concerning STD/HIV. Schools, businesses, and government agencies sometimes develop policies and laws concerning STD/HIV. You should be alert to any legislation being proposed, and make your opinions known to officials and legislators. All people can support and promote HIV education, research, and health care.

Financial resources are needed to help stop the spread of STD/HIV. Funds can help many projects, such as educational programs and medical research. More health care services are needed. Support services for persons with AIDS, particularly, are valuable. One could help organize and/or support fund-raising drives through a club or similar group.

5. Support a Friend with STD/HIV. Persons infected with STD/HIV sometimes need support and even help. This is particularly true for persons infected with an incurable STD, such as AIDS and genital herpes. Many persons with AIDS have been mistreated. Some have lost jobs and homes. Others have been denied medical and social services. Still others have been rejected by family, friends, and co-workers. Hence, many persons with AIDS have felt isolated and emotionally distressed. Friends can be very valuable. If a friend of yours develops an STD, such as AIDS, continue sharing activities and conversation. The friend may want to discuss worries and concerns. Listen. Remember, you cannot get STD/HIV by being near to someone infected with STD/HIV or who has AIDS. You can hug the person and hold his or her hand.

The families of persons with AIDS also need help. They may be living with the fact that their loved one is dying. Concerned friends can be very valuable to these families.

Conclusion

Millions of persons suffer physical and emotional health problems from STD/HIV. STD/HIV are dangerous, but infections are easy to prevent. The organisms that cause STD/HIV are passed almost entirely by actions you can choose to avoid. You, and persons like you, can prevent STD/HIV. How? Make responsible choices and decisions for yourself.

— — — — — — — —

Check-up: (Write here only if you can keep this book.)

1. People's actions are the most important factors in reducing the spread of STD/HIV.   TRUE   FALSE

2. What is the best way you can help prevent the spread of STD/HIV? _____

_____

3. Where can you get information about STD/HIV? _____

_____

4. What are some ways you can help promote STD/HIV prevention? _____

_____

Answers to Check-up:

1. TRUE. A person's preventive health behaviors are the most important factors in reducing the spread of STD/HIV.
2. Accepting responsibility for your health and the health of any sex partners is the best way you can help stop STD/HIV.
3. Parents or guardians, religious leaders, teachers, school nurses, counselors, health departments, STD/HIV clinics, and doctors are important sources of STD/HIV information. Also, the National STD Hotline and the National AIDS Hotline can be called.
4. You can help promote STD/HIV prevention efforts by (1)serving as a responsible role model, (2) promoting healthy peer norms, (3) serving as an accurate information source, (4) supporting STD/HIV control efforts, and (5) supporting a friend with STD/HIV.

What Do You Think? (Answer these questions in your mind. Don't write them anywhere.)

1. Are most young people responsible enough for their own health to keep themselves, and any sex partners, free from STD/HIV? Why?
2. Should a person be required to take STD/HIV tests when he/she gets a routine physical examination? Should a woman be required to take STD/HIV tests during a Pap test or pelvic examination?
3. Is STD/HIV education needed, or is it a waste of time? For example, should STD/HIV be discussed at school, on radio and television, and in the newspapers?
4. If a friend told you that he/she had an STD, such as AIDS, how could you be supportive and understanding? Could you continue being friends?

Life Situation #6 (Try solving this problem before reading the answer.)

Lupe is a member of an STD/HIV teenage speaker's bureau from his school. A friend from another school that does not have much STD/HIV education asked him to make a presentation to a club. The main topic he chose to speak about is how each person, individually, can help control STD/HIV.

QUESTION: What are the most important things Lupe could say? (See page 61 for the answer.)

Possible Solutions to Life Situations

1. No, they do not realize that STD/HIV are a serious health problem in our country. There are many statistics presented in STD/HIV FACT #1 on page 11 that you could give them concerning the size and consequence of the problem. Basically, you could tell them that STD/HIV are very common in the United States. Over 40 million persons, including babies, are affected. STD/HIV cause more serious damage to teenagers than all other communicable diseases combined. Every 13 seconds a teenager gets an STD. STD/HIV cases are found everywhere, including small towns and rural areas, suburbs and large cities. STD/HIV can lead to serious health problems that include damage to the reproductive system, the nervous system, and may even lead to death.

2. Jennifer should first state that STD/HIV are passed (1) during sexual contact with an infected person, (2) by infected blood in injecting drug equipment, and (3) from an infected mother to her child. Jennifer then can tell Kelly that sexual abstinence and not sharing injecting drug equipment are the surest ways of avoiding STD/HIV. Uninfected partners who practice mutual monogamy in a long-term, steady relationship or marriage will not get STD HIV through sexual contact. People with different partners increase their risk of STD/HIV infection. For persons with different partners, use of the latex condom greatly reduces the chance of infection, although it is not 100% effective. A person should also avoid sexual contact with persons who might be at high risk for having STD/HIV. Jennifer could also inform Kelly about the major STD/HIV symptoms and how to get STD/HIV counseling and medical care.

3. James did one correct thing. He stopped having sex after the blisters appeared. However, he should have stopped because of the chance of passing on a disease, not just because the sores were too painful. James failed to do three important things. First, he should have gone to a doctor quickly and asked for STD/HIV tests. Secondly, he should have been sure that all of his sex partners saw a doctor. Lastly, he should not have started having sex again. James did not know the symptoms of STD/HIV infection very well. He didn't realize that the symptoms of many STD/HIV disappear on their own. But, the person can still have an STD and pass it on. And, James didn't understand that for many females the symptoms of STD are not easily noticed. Thomasina may have had the same blisters, but may not have noticed them.

4. Maria should call the local health department. Many towns have public STD or HIV/AIDS clinics run by the health department. The health department is usually listed in the telephone book yellow pages under county or city government offices. Sometimes, it is listed in the white pages under "health," or in the blue pages of government listings. If your town does not have a clinic, the local health department can still help you find medical care. Finally, Maria could call the National STD Hotline or the National AIDS Hotline for the address of the nearest clinic. Maria needs to know that teenagers can get STD/HIV medical care in every state without their parents' permission. Also, many clinics will treat a person with an STD for free if money is a problem. To help Maria deal with her feelings, you could tell her that STDs are very common and that people who get STDs aren't bad people. They have illnesses caused by organisms. All types of people get STD/HIV. STD/HIV are not punishment for sexual activity. The most important thing is for Maria and her partner to be treated quickly and to avoid STD/HIV in the future.

5. Kevin should have talked with Pat as soon as possible after discovering he had an HIV infection. He did not realize that it sometimes takes several years for an HIV infection to develop into AIDS. It is important that Pat be informed soon about a possible HIV infection. Then, Pat can receive medical care and, hopefully, avoid passing HIV to others. In talking with Pat, Kevin could admit that what he is going to say is not easy. He should encourage Pat to see a doctor as soon as possible. Kevin should point out that tests and treatment are confidential, and that some clinics even have anonymous testing. Then, he could have offered to go with Pat to a doctor or clinic. If Kevin could not have talked with Pat, he could have asked the doctor or clinic to notify Pat. A STD/HIV case specialist would then contact Pat, and Kevin's name would never be mentioned.

6. Lupe could tell the club members that being responsible for their own health, and the health of any sex or drug-use partners, is the best way a person can help control STD/HIV. He could continue by stating that being responsible means: (1) avoiding STD/HIV yourself; (2) paying close attention to your body and your partner's body for STD/HIV symptoms; (3) seeking medical care if an STD/HIV infection is suspected; (4) not passing STD/HIV on to others; and (5) being sure to get sex partners to a doctor if you get an STD. Details about each of the five suggestions should follow. For example, it would be good to describe STD/HIV prevention measures and symptoms. In conclusion, because their school does not teach much about STD/HIV, Lupe could inform them of other STD/HIV information sources.

I Learned That...

DIRECTIONS: This activity can help you review some of the major facts about STD/HIV. Write in what you learned about each topic below. You might want to check your response with information in the STD/HIV Summary Sheet on page 98.

1. About ways STD/HIV are transmitted, I learned that:

2. About how to avoid STD/HIV, I learned that:

3. About how to recognize STD/HIV symptoms, I learned that :

4. About what to do after recognizing STD/HIV symptoms or suspecting an infection, I learned that:

5. About how to get sex and injecting drug use partners to treatment, I learned that :

6. Where to get STD/HIV information and help, I learned that :

7. About ways I can promote STD/HIV prevention efforts, I
   learned that:

STD/HIV PREVENTION ACTION CHECKLIST

Listed below are the behavioral goals of this book. They stress what you can do now and later to avoid STD/HIV. You do *not* have to check any of these actions. But you can use the list to remind yourself of the ways you can help control STD/HIV.

To help stop STD/HIV, I will:

___avoid sexual exposure to STD/HIV.

___not use injecting drugs or share needles.

___resist peer pressure to practice risky behaviors.

___recognize early symptoms of an STD/HIV infection.

___avoid exposing others if an STD/HIV infection is diagnosed or suspected.

___seek prompt medical care if an STD/HIV infection is suspected.

___follow a physician's directions if treated for STD/HIV.

___get all sex and drug-use partners to medical care if one has STD/ HIV.

___be supportive and helpful to persons infected with STD/HIV.

___serve as an accurate source of STD/HIV information and advice.

___serve as a positive role model to others.

___promote healthy behavior among peers.

___seek the help of others concerning STD/HIV issues.

___promote STD/HIV education, research, and health care.

STD/HIV AVOIDANCE SKILLS

As stated earlier, young adults may face pressures to participate in STD/HIV risky activities. A person needs many skills to resist the pressure and to avoid STD/HIV. These skills can be learned, although it may take much practice over several years. To help you become better at some of the STD/HIV avoidance skills, a few of them are addressed below. Certainly the activities do not address all of the skills you need. However, there are other ways you can develop your avoidance skills. For example, school lessons about other health areas and teaching from your parents and other adults are important. Ask the people you trust to help you become better at STD/HIV avoidance skills.

The activities are not required. But, you will probably find them fun and valuable.

ACTIVITY #1: BEING RESPONSIBLE FOR STD/HIV PREVENTION

Being responsible for STD/HIV prevention involves many facets. This activity deals with two: (1) talking about prevention with a dating partner with whom you may have sexual contact, and (2) avoiding unwanted behavior.

PART A: TALKING ABOUT PREVENTION

1. When a person is trying to talk with a dating partner about STD/HIV prevention, the opening line is sometimes the most difficult. Create one or two opening statements that could be used to get the talk started. _____

_____

_____

_____

2. When talking about STD/HIV prevention, one might need to clearly state his or her values. That is, an assertive — not passive — statement should be made. Create one or two assertive statements concerning avoiding STD/HIV with a dating partner. (Example of an assertive statement: "I will not have sexual intercourse." Example of passive statement: "Even though I am not sure I am ready, I guess we can have sexual intercourse if you really want to.") _____

_____

_____

_____

3. If a dating partner agrees to practice STD/HIV prevention, it would be good to reinforce his or her decision. What could a person say to a dating partner to praise his or her decision?

_____

_____

_____

_____

4. Sometimes, a dating partner or others will continue to pressure a person to participate in risky behavior despite the person's refusal. One way to deal with the situation would be to leave. This may be difficult because the person does not want to lose the dating partner or friend. What could be said if he or she decides to leave the situation, yet the person wants to maintain the relationship with the dating partner?

_____

_____

_____

_____

5. Practice the above statements with a friend.

PART B: UNWANTED BEHAVIOR

1. In what situations might unwanted sexual behavior or drug use be more likely to occur? _____

_____

_____

2. How can a person express love and affection without having sexual intercourse? List some ways.

_____

_____

_____

ACTIVITY #2: FORMING ONE'S SEXUAL CODE OF BEHAVIOR

One aspect of becoming a mature person is developing a personal sexual code of behavior. That is, each person needs to establish limits to the type of sexual behavior he/she will participate in and with whom the person will have sexual contact. To help you do this, answer the questions below:

1. What should be considered when forming one's sexual code of behavior. (Example: family values, religion, and age).

_____

_____

_____

2. Who can help a person form and maintain a sexual code of behavior?

_____

_____

_____

3. What can a person do to reinforce his or her chosen sexual code of behavior? (Example: avoid situations that pressure one to violate the sexual code).

_____

_____

_____

ACTIVITY #3: OPPOSING PRESSURE LINES

Most young adults will at some time be pressured by others to participate in STD/HIV risky behaviors. They may do this by trying to talk you into doing something you do not want to do. One way you can resist this pressure is to be ready with a response.

Create a refusal or opposing statement for each of the pressure statements given below. An example is given to help you understand the activity. Once you have completed the activity, practice using the lines with a friend. Also, you may want to ask someone else to help you create the opposing line.

Pressure Line 1
If you really cared about me, you would have sex with me. Gosh, we have been dating for a long time.
Opposing Statement
You are right. I care about you and we have been together for a long time. Sex may seem right for you, but I'm not going to be rushed into it. I'm going to wait until it's the right thing for me.

Pressure Line 2
Everyone our age is having sex.
Opposing Statement

_____

_____

_____

Pressure Line 3
I'll quit dating you if we don't have sex.
Opposing Statement

_____

_____

_____

Pressure Line 4
Using a condom for sex is too much trouble.
Opposing Statement

_____

_____

_____

Pressure Line 5
The only real way to get high is to use drugs.
Opposing Statement

_____

_____

_____

ACTIVITY #4: FAMILY VALUES

Parents or guardians can play an important role in helping a person form good health values. They can be very helpful in teaching responsible health decisions. It is valuable to talk about sexual issues with a parent or trusted adult. When this occurs, the young adult usually makes more responsible decisions.

This activity is designed to assist you, your parents or guardians, or trusted adults to talk about sexuality, drugs, and STD/HIV. If for some reason you cannot talk with a parent, discuss the questions with a trusted adult. Together with your parents or trusted adult, answer the questions below. The response may be written after each question.

70

1. What can be gained from parents and their children discussing sexuality and STD/HIV together? _____

_____

_____

2. What can be done to increase the likelihood that young adults and their parents would talk about sexuality and STD/HIV?

_____

_____

3. What are the sexual issues that are important for young adults and their parents to discuss? _____

_____

_____

4. What are your family's values about sexuality and young adults? _____

_____

_____

ACTIVITY #5: FINDING STD/HIV HELP IN THE TELEPHONE BOOK

You may need more information or health services related to STD/HIV. Most communities have STD/HIV help available. But, you may not know where to call. Although there may be several sources of help, contacting the health department is usually the best step. If the health department cannot help you, they can suggest who can.

DIRECTIONS: With another person, such as a friend, locate the local health department number in the telephone book. The health department is usually listed in the city or county government numbers. Sometimes the health department is listed in the white pages under "health" or in the blue pages of government listings. Call the health department and ask about sources of STD/HIV information, where STD/HIV counseling and testing are located, and if there is a local STD or AIDS/HIV hotline. Write the information on the form located on the inside back cover of this book. (NOTE: If the health department cannot be easily located in the telephone book, call the information operator. Also, a crisis telephone hotline can be helpful.)

SELF-TEST
Discovering What I Know-2

These questions are similar to the ones given in the front of the book. By answering them, you can see if your knowledge about STD/HIV has improved. Use another sheet if you cannot keep this book. Again, you are *not* required to answer these questions.

Answer Key: T = True, F = False

T F   1. STD/HIV cases are a problem only in large cities.

T F   2. Young people do not need to worry about HIV infection.

T F   3. Sexual intercourse is the most common way STD/HIV are transmitted.

T F   4. One cannot get HIV from *donating* blood.

T F   5. Sexual abstinence is the surest way of avoiding STD/HIV.

T F   6. Mutual monogamy greatly reduces the chances of getting STD/HIV.

T F   7. Not using injecting drugs helps one avoid HIV.

T F   8. STD/HIV symptoms are sometimes absent or not easily noticed.

T F   9. STD/HIV can be passed to others only when symptoms of infection are present.

T F   10. Young adults who have engaged in high-risk behavior can get confidential STD/HIV counseling and treatment.

T F   11. A person can learn where to get STD/HIV counseling and treatment by calling the local health department.

T F   12. All STDs can be cured.

T F 13. The government — not each person — should have the main role for controlling STD/HIV.

ANSWERS: The correct answers are given below. Look up any questions you missed using the page numbers listed below.

1. F (p.12) 5. T (p.22) 9. F (p.33) 13. F (p.51)
2. F (p.12) 6. T (p.22) 10. T (p.38)
3. T (p.18) 7. T (p.24) 11. T (p.38)
4. T (p.20) 8. T (p.33) 12. F (p.41)

SELF-TEST
Discovering What I Believe - 2

These statements are the same as the ones in the front of the book. It might be fun to see if your beliefs have changed. Circle the letter D or A for each statement below that is most like what you think. Use another sheet if you cannot keep this book. Your responses will *not* affect your grade. You are *not* required to take this quiz.

ANSWER KEY: D = disagree, A = agree

D A 1. People are making too big a deal out of STD/HIV.
D A 2. People get infected with STD/HIV because they are being punished for their wrong actions.
D A 3. Practicing sexual abstinence to avoid STD/HIV is taking the STD/HIV problem too seriously.
D A 4. Using condoms to prevent STD/HIV is too much trouble.

D A 5. Persons infected with STD/HIV don't have any obligation to get their sex partners to a doctor.

D A 6. STD/HIV doctors and health care workers cannot be trusted.

D A 7. Anyone with an STD/HIV infection who gives the name of a sex partner to the doctor is a "squealer."

D A 8. People with an STD/HIV infection do not deserve help from others, since they get what they deserve.

D A 9. Students with an STD/HIV infection should not be permitted in school.

D A 10. It is best to stop being friends with someone who has STD/HIV.

D A 11. STD/HIV infection should be the concern of other cities and towns, but not mine.

D A 12. STD/HIV education in schools is a waste of time.

RESULTS: If you decided:

D Your beliefs help control STD/HIV

A You lack an understanding about STD/HIV prevention.

Female Reproductive System

Description of Each Part

ANUS (ANE-us). The rear opening of the digestive tract through which bulk waste (feces) passes out of the body.

BLADDER (BLAD-er). The sac where urine is stored until it leaves the body.

CERVIX (SIR-vicks). Lower part of the uterus which extends into the vagina.

CLITORIS (KLIT-or-iss). Small sensitive organ located at the top of the labia.

FALLOPIAN TUBE (fah-LOW-pee-un). A hollow tube through which eggs travel from the ovary to the uterus.

MAJOR LIP or Outer Labia (LAY-be-uh). The larger and more outer lip-like structures that covers the opening of the vagina.

MINOR LIP or Inner Labia (LAY-be-uh). The smaller and inner lip-like structures that cover the opening of the vagina.

OVARY (OH-vuh-ree). One of the two female organs that secrete female hormones and produce ova (eggs).

PUBIC HAIR (PYOU-bick). Hair that grows around the sex organs.

RECTUM (REK-tum). The lowest part of the large intestines.

URETHRA (your-EETH-ruh). The tube through which urine passes out of the body.

UTERUS (YOU-ter-us). Organ where the fertilized egg becomes implanted and develops into a baby. Also called "womb."

VAGINA (va-JINE-uh). The female birth canal and tube that accepts the penis during intercourse.

External structures

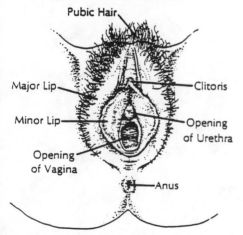

76

External and internal structures: side view

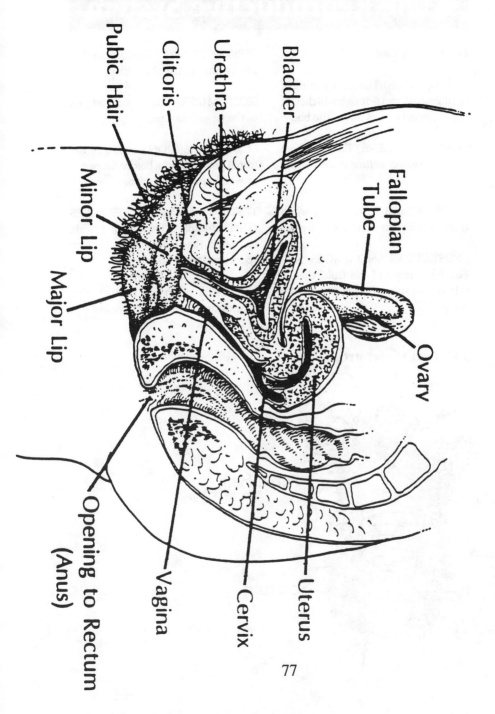

Pubic Hair

Clitoris

Urethra

Bladder

Fallopian
Tube

Minor Lip

Major Lip

Ovary

Opening to Rectum
(Anus)

Vagina

Cervix

Uterus

Male Reproductive System

Description of Each Part

ANUS (ANE-us). The rear opening of the digestive tract through which bulk waste (feces) passes out of the body.

BLADDER (BLAD-er). The sac where urine is stored before it leaves the body.

PENIS (PEE-nis). The male sex organ through which urine and semen pass.

PROSTATE GLAND (PROSS-tate). Furnishes most of the fluid that is mixed with sperm before it leaves the body.

PUBIC HAIR (PYOU-bick). Hair that grows around the sex organs.

RECTUM (REK-tum). The lowest part of the large intestines.

SCROTUM (SKROH-tum). The external pouch of skin, below the penis, in which the testes are contained.

TESTES (TEHS-tees) or TESTICLES (TEHS-ti-kuhls). Two male glands located in the scrotum that produce sperm and male hormones.

URETHRA (yoor-EETH-ruh). The tube through which urine passes out of the body.

External view: front

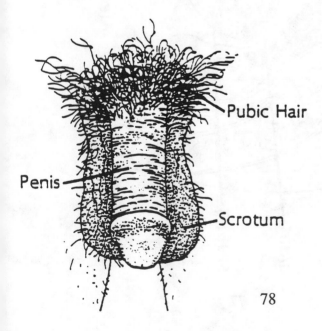

Pubic Hair

Penis

Scrotum

External and internal structures: side view

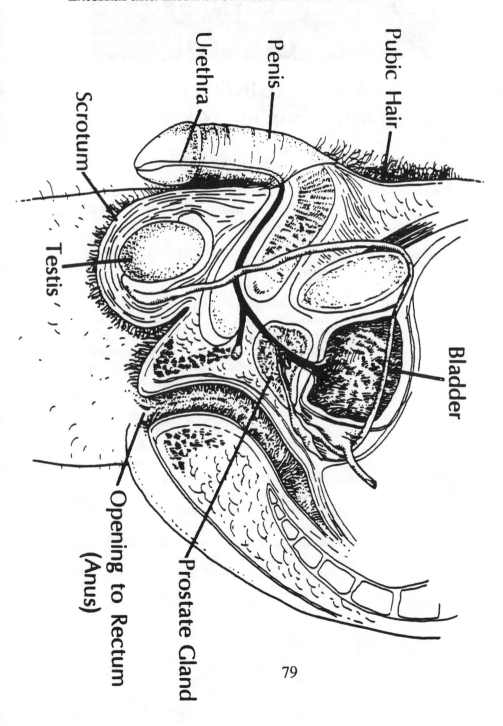

Urethra

Penis

Pubic Hair

Scrotum

Testis

Bladder

Opening to Rectum (Anus)

Prostate Gland

79

SUMMARY CHARTS OF IMPORTANT STDs

CHLAMYDIAL INFECTIONS
(klah-MID-ee-ul in-FECK-shuns)

Other Names:
Chlamydia: *Chlamydia trachomatis.*

Organism:
Bacteria: *Chlamydia trachomatis.* Passed during sexual contact; infants become infected during vaginal delivery. Highly contagious.

Incubation:
2-3 weeks for males; usually no symptoms in females.

Typical Symptoms:
Symptoms may develop slowly and are often mild. Many cases have no symptoms. **Females:** sometimes a slight vaginal discharge; itching and burning of vagina, painful intercourse; bleeding between menstrual periods; abdominal pain; fever in later stages. **Males:** discharge from penis; burning and itching in the urethra; pain and swelling in the testicles; slight fever; burning sensation during urination.

Diagnosis:
May be difficult to diagnose, but culture test can determine disease. Test involves using a swab to collect a small amount of fluid from infected body part. Diagnosis is sometimes done by ruling out gonorrhea with appropriate tests. A more rapid test involving microscopic examination of discharge from urethra or cervix has been recently developed. This test may be available in some clinics.

Treatment:	Curable with antibiotics (not penicillin).
Danger:	If untreated can cause pelvic inflammatory disease, sterility, premature and still births, and infant pneumonia and eye infections which can lead to blindness.
Comments:	Widespread in USA with an estimated 4 million people getting the disease annually. About one-half of nongonococcal urethritis in men and pelvic inflammatory disease in women has been attributed to chlamydia. Many persons with gonorrhea also have chlamydia.

GENITAL HERPES
(JEN-a-tul HERP-eez)

Other Names:	Herpes simplex virus (HSV).
Organism:	Virus: *Herpes virus hominis*. Virus can be found anywhere on the body, but is usually found on the genital area. Passed by direct contact with infectious blisters or sores usually found on the genitals, anus, or mouth.
Incubation:	From a few days to about 3 weeks.
Typical Symptoms:	Formation of painful blisters or sores on the genitals, rectum, or mouth that break, crust over, and heal in 2-4 weeks. Females may have sores on the cervix without pain. Sores may reappear throughout life, although they heal faster and occur less frequently with time. Factors like stress, fatigue, and other illnesses may trigger recurrence of sores in some people.
Diagnosis:	Visual examination, tissue culture, Pap smear, and microscopic slide examination of fluid from sore.

81

Treatment:	No medicine can cure herpes at the present time; medications are sometimes given to relieve pain, to shorten the time of sores, or to prevent bacterial infections at the open sores.
Danger:	Women with HSV may have a greater risk of developing cancer of the cervix (these women should get a Pap test every year). Herpes can be fatal to infants who acquire the disease, and many other infants suffer permanent brain damage. If the mother has an active case at the time of birth, the baby can be protected by Caesarian delivery.
Comments:	There are an estimated 30 million genital herpes cases in the USA, with one-half million new cases each year. Infected persons should avoid intimate contact with others when blisters or sores are present. Genital herpes has been found to be related to an increased risk of acquiring HIV. The American Social Health Association has developed a service for persons with herpes infections, called the Herpes Resource Center. It provides self-help support groups and a quarterly newsletter. For more information, write to: Herpes Resource Center, Box 13827, Research Triangle Park, North Carolina 27709. Call 919-361-8488 during weekdays between 9:00 a.m. and 7:00 p.m.

GENITAL WARTS (JEN-a-tul WORTS)

Other Names:	Venereal warts; condyloma acuminata.
Organism:	Human papillomavirus. Transmitted by direct contact with warts in the genital and anal area.
Incubation:	6 weeks to 8 months.

Typical Symptoms:	Some persons may not have symptoms. Others have warty growths around genital and anal area, and sometimes in the throat.
Diagnosis:	Usually identified by observation of warts. Biopsy (skin examined under microscope) might be done in some cases.
Treatment:	Medication applied to warts, freezing or laser therapy, or surgical removal. Treatment may not be completely effective. Warts may reappear.
Danger:	Can grow to large size and obstruct vagina, urethra, or anus. Can be transmitted to infant during birth. Some recent studies have suggested an association between certain human papillomaviruses and cervical cancer. Yearly Pap smears are essential for women with warts.
Comments:	One of the most common STDs with an estimated 12 million cases. Persons with genital warts should get periodic medical check-ups.

GONORRHEA (GON-oh-REE-ah)

Other Names:	GC, clap, drip.
Organism:	Bacteria: *Neisseria gonorrhoeae.* Typically passed by direct contact between the infectious mucous membranes, e.g., genitals, anus, and mouth, of one person and the mucous membranes of another. Contaminated fingers can pass the organism from infected mucous membranes to the eyes. Acquiring disease from objects is very unlikely.
Incubation:	Usually 2-10 days, but possibly 30 days or more.

83

Typical Symptoms:	Genitals (penis or cervix), anus, throat, and eyes can be infected. **Males:** burning urination and pus discharge for infection of urethra (5-20% have no symptoms). **Females:** may have vaginal discharge, although up to 80% have no symptoms for cervical infection. **Both sexes:** mucous discharge from anus, blood and pus in feces, irritation of anus or infection of rectum; often no symptoms or mild sore throat for gonorrhea of the throat. Infection of eyes is rare in adults.
Diagnosis:	Microscopic examination of discharge; culture from possible infection site.
Treatment:	Curable with antibiotics.
Danger:	Pelvic inflammatory disease (PID), sterility in both sexes, arthritis, blindness, meningitis, heart damage, kidney damage, skin rash, ectopic pregnancy, and eye damage in newborns (acquired from mother's vagina during child birth).
Comments:	Number one reportable communicable disease in the United States with an estimated 750 thousand cases yearly. PID occurs in about 15% of females infected. Gonorrhea is a major cause of sterility, particularly in women. Some gonorrhea strains have become more resistant to penicillin and other antibiotics in recent years. However, all types of gonorrhea are treatable by some type of antibiotic.

HEPATITIS (hep-uh-TITE-us)

Organism:	Virus: Hepatitis A or B. Virus found in saliva, blood, semen, urine, and feces. Passed by sexual contact including anal or oral sex. Can be passed nonsexually from shared razors, toothbrushes, needles, eating utensils, and

84

other similar objects. Hepatitis A can be passed from food or water that contains fecal material.

Incubation:	Hepatitis A: 15-50 days. Hepatitis B: 45-160 days.
Typical Symptoms:	Some persons may not have any symptoms. Others have nausea, fever, loss of appetite, dark "cola-colored" urine, abdominal discomfort, jaundice, yellow eyes, and enlarged liver.
Diagnosis:	Blood test.
Treatment:	No medical cure. Most persons recover within 6 to 8 weeks. Bed rest, good nutrition, and avoidance of alcohol and drugs are recommended.
Danger:	Can cause severe illness, liver damage, and death; premature birth or spontaneous abortion; infant may be born with Hepatitis B acquired from mother.
Comments:	At least one-half million persons affected annually. Hepatitis A can be prevented or lessened by an injection of immune serum globulin within 2 weeks following exposure. Homosexual males have a high risk for Hepatitis B. A vaccine for Hepatitis B is now available.

HIV Infection and AIDS

Other Names:	*Human immunodeficiency virus* (HYOO-men im-Yoon-oh-de-FISH-un-see VY-rus) or the virus that causes AIDS, and acquired immunodeficiency syndrome (uh-CHOIR-d im YOON-oh-de-FISH-un-see SIN-drome).

Organism:	Virus transmitted through sexual contact, contaminated injecting drug equipment, and an infected mother to her child during pregnancy, childbirth, or breast-feeding. HIV attacks the body's immune system, its natural defense against disease.
Incubation:	Ranges from a few months to ten years or more.
Typical Symptoms:	Symptoms of HIV-infected persons can include tiredness, swollen lymph glands, fever, loss of appetite and weight, diarrhea, and night sweats. Most persons infected with HIV have periods of both health and illness. However, over time the symptoms may become more frequent and severe.
Diagnosis:	The presence of HIV is established by a blood test that detects antibodies to HIV. HIV-infected persons may acquire certain severe illnesses, which usually classify them as having AIDS.
Treatment:	There is no cure or vaccine for HIV infection or AIDS. Some newer drugs inhibit the growth of HIV and the patient may have periods of fairly healthy life. However, the person still has HIV and can still die from AIDS.
Danger:	Over 50 percent of persons with AIDS in the USA have died, many within two years after diagnosis of AIDS. No one has completely recovered from AIDS.
Comments:	Many persons infected with HIV do not know about their infection. Most AIDS cases have been homosexual and bisexual males. There is an increasing proportion of total AIDS cases occurring among teenagers, injecting drug users, women, and heterosexuals.

PEDICULOSIS PUBIS
(pa-DIK-you-LO-sis PUE-bus)

Other Names: Crabs, pubic lice, and cooties.

Organism: Louse: *Phthirus pubis*. Passed by direct contact with infested person or by infested sheets, towels, and clothing.

Incubation: Eggs hatch after 3 to 14 days.

Typical Symptoms: Some persons may not have any symptoms. Others have intense itching, blue or gray spots, and insects or nits (eggs) in the pubic area. Also may have pinhead-size blood spots on underwear.

Diagnosis: Microscopic examination of nits on hair and locating adult lice adhering to hair.

Treatment: Cured with special creams, lotions, or shampoos that can be bought at drugstores. Some products require a prescription while others do not (ask the pharmacist for the correct product).

Danger: None.

Comments: To prevent getting the disease again, treatment of sex partner is necessary. Further, clothing and bed sheets should be thoroughly cleaned.

SYPHILIS (SIF-i-liss)

Other Names: Syph, bad blood, the pox

Organism: Bacteria: *Treponema pallidum*. Passed by direct contact with infectious sores or rashes.

Incubation: Ten days to 3 months, with average of 21 days.

Typical Symptoms: **Primary stage**: painless chancre (sore) at site of entry of germ and swollen glands. **Secondary stage**: symptoms usually appear 1 week to 6 months after appearance of chancre and may include rash, patchy hair loss, sore throat, and swollen glands. Primary and secondary sores will go away even without treatment, but the germs continue to spread throughout the body. **Latent syphilis**: may continue 5-20 years or more with no symptoms, but the person is no longer infectious to other people. A pregnant woman can transmit the disease to her unborn child. **Late syphilis**: varies from no symptoms to indications of damage to body organs such as the brain and heart.

Diagnosis: Physical examination, microscope slide from sore, blood tests.

Treatment: Easily cured with antibiotics.

Danger: Severe damage to nervous system and other body organs possible after many years: heart disease, insanity, brain damage, and severe illness or death of newborns.

Comments: Symptoms may imitate those of other diseases; damage done to body is permanent; treatment of pregnant women with syphilis is necessary to prevent damage to fetus.

TRICHOMONIASIS
(TRIK-uh-moe-NYE-uh-sis)

Other Name: Trich.

Organism: Protozoan: *Trichomonas vaginalis.* Usually passed by direct sexual contact. Can also be transmitted through contact with wet objects, such as towels, washcloths, and douching equipment.

Incubation: 4 to 20 days, with average being 7 days.

Typical Symptoms: Some women and most men have no symptoms. **Females:** white or greenish-yellow odorous discharge; vaginal itching and soreness, painful urination. **Males:** slight itching of penis, painful urination, clear discharge from penis.

Diagnosis: Microscopic slide of discharge; culture test; examination.

Treatment: Curable with oral medication.

Danger: Long-term effects in adults not known. There is some evidence that infected individuals are more likely to develop cervical cancer. Babies may become infected.

Comments: Very common.

PRONOUNCING GLOSSARY

abdominal (ab-DOM-i-nul). In the belly or stomach area.

AIDS. The initials for the illness acquired immunodeficiency syndrome.

anal intercourse (A-null IN-ter-course). Sexual union involving the penis in the rectum.

anonymous (uh-NON-uh-mus). The person's identity is unknown.

antibody (ANN-ti-bah-dee). Substance in the blood produced by the immune system. Antibodies destroy germs that enter the body.

bacteria (bac-TEER-ee-uh). Living, one-celled microorganisms . Some may cause disease while others are beneficial.

bisexual (by-SEK-shoo-ul). Sexual attraction and interest directed toward both females and males.

blood transfusion. The injection of blood into another person.

casual contact (KAZ-you-ul KON-takt). Non-sexual body contact including touching, hugging, handshaking, and sitting closely together.

cervix (SIR-vicks). The lower opening of the uterus (or womb) in the female.

communicable disease (kom-UNE-ik-ah-bl di-zeez). Diseases that can be passed along from person to person. Caused by bacteria, viruses, and other organisms.

condom (KON-dom). A rubber cover or sheath worn over the penis. Used during sexual activity to prevent STD/HIV and pregnancy.

confidential (kon-fa-DEN-shul). Secret or private matters; no one else is told.

diagnose (die-ag-NOS). Identifying which disease a patient has.

ectopic pregnancy (ek-TOP-ik PREG-nun-see). The implantation of a fertilized egg outside of uterus, usually in the fallopian tube.

genitals (JEN-a-tulz). The external sex organs.

heterosexual (HET-eh-row-SEK-shoo-ul). Sexual attraction and interest directed toward the other sex.

HIV. The initials for *human immunodeficiency virus*, the cause of AIDS.

HIV-infected person. A person having HIV.

homosexual (HO-muh-SEK-shoo-ul). Sexual attraction and interest directed toward the same sex.

illicit drugs (ih-LIS-it). Illegal drugs, such as heroin.

immune system (im-YOON). A body system that fights germs that enter the body.

immunity (im-YOON-ih-tee). Protection from acquiring a disease.

incubation period (in-kew-BAY-shun). The period between when a person is first exposed to a disease and when the symptoms appear.

infection (in-FECK-shun). A disease caused by germs, such as viruses and bacteria.

injecting drug . A drug injected by needles into a person's veins.

injecting drug equipment. Devices used to inject drugs, mainly syringes and needles.

lesbian (LEZ-bee-un). A female homosexual.

mutually monogamous (muh-NAHG-uh-mus). A relationship in which the two people have sex only with each other.

91

opportunistic disease (OP-poor-tune-IS-tic). A disease or infection acquired by persons whose immune system is weakened or damaged by HIV. A healthy immune system usually can fight off the disease or infection.

oral-anal sex (OR-el—A-null). Touching a partner's anus with the mouth.

oral-genital sex (OR-el—JEN-a-tul). Touching a partner's genitals with the mouth. Also, commonly called "oral sex."

pelvic inflammatory disease (PEL-vik-in-FLAM-uh-tor-ee). An infection in females of the pelvic organs, such as the uterus and fallopian tubes. Also called PID.

penis (PEE-nis). The male sex organ through which semen and urine pass.

prostitute (PRAHS-tih-toot). A person who receives money for having sex with someone.

protozoan (PRO-ta-ZOH-an). A simple one-celled animal that chiefly lives in water. Can be seen only with a microscope.

public health specialist. A person from the STD clinic, HIV/AIDS clinic, or health department who provides STD/HIV information to patients and who is trained to locate sex partners of a person with an STD.

rectum (REK-tum). The lowest part of the large intestines.

resistant (ree-ZISS-tant). In reference to disease organisms, the organisms become so strong that some drugs will not destroy them.

risk reduction. Individual actions designed to decrease the chances of harming one's health.

risky behavior. Individual actions that might lead to harming one's health.

semen (SEE-men). The fluid that is expelled from the penis during sex.

92

sexual abstinence (AB-sta-nence). Not having sex with another person.

sexual code of behavior. The rules used by a person in determining which sexual behaviors he or she will participate in and which ones he or she will avoid.

sexual intercourse. Sexual union involving the penis and the vagina. The union of the penis and anus (anal intercourse) and union of the penis and mouth (oral intercourse) are considered sexual intercourse by some.

sexual orientation (OR-ee-in-TAY-shun). Whether a person is bisexual, heterosexual, or homosexual.

sexually transmitted diseases (SEK-shoo-ul-ee TRANS-mit-ed di-ZEEZ-es). Diseases most often passed from person to person through sexual contact.

signs. Measured or objective evidence of a disease as determined by a physician.

STDs. The initials for "sexually transmitted diseases."

sterility (stuh-RILL-i-tee). Not being able to become a father or mother because of damaged parts of the reproductive system.

symptoms (SIMP-tums). Subjective evidence of an illness. Changes in a person's health that can be seen or felt.

syringe (suh-RINJ). A medical instrument used to inject fluids into the body.

transmitted (TRANS-mit-ed). Passed along from one person or place to another.

urethritis (yoor-eeth-RIGHT-us). Infection of the urethra, the tube through which urine passes out of the body.

vaccine (VAK-seen). Weakened or killed disease organisms given to people to prevent an infectious disease.

vagina (va-jINE-uh). Also called the birth canal. The tube that leads from a woman's uterus (womb) to the outside of her body.

vaginal fluids (VAJ-eh-nul). Fluids within the vagina produced by the female reproductive glands.

vaginal intercourse (VAJ-eh-nul). Sexual union involving the penis in the vagina, commonly called "sexual intercourse."

values (VAL-yoos). A strongly held belief or principle.

venereal disease (VD) (vuh-NEAR-ee-ul di-ZEEZ). A general term describing certain diseases that are transmitted during sexual contact.

virus (VY-rus). A small organism that can cause disease.

wart (WORT). Raised growth, usually hard and dry, caused by a virus.

Index

I
illicit drugs, 19
immune system, 30
immunity, 18
incubation period, 13
insects, 21
injecting drugs, 13, 15, 19, 24
injecting drug equipment, 19

K
kissing, 19

L
lesbian, 19

M
minors, 37-38
monogamy (mutual), 22
mosquitos, 21
multiple sex partners, 19

N
needles, 19, 24

O
opportunistic diseases, 30-31
oral-anal sex, 18
oral-genital sex, 18

P
parents, 28, 37, 53
partner
    referral, 42, 46-49
    selection, 23-24
pediculosis pubis, 11, 20, 87
peer
    norms, 54
    pressure, 27, 54
pelvic inflammatory
  disease (PID), 10, 14
penis, 19, 23, 78-79
pubic lice (see pediculosis pubis)

public health specialist, 47-48
pregnancy, 25
prostitutes, 15, 24

R
rectum, 19, 76-79
reinfection, 46-47
resistant, 15
risky behavior, 9, 18-20
risk reduction, 21-25
role model, 54

S
saliva, 19, 21
semen, 19, 22, 25
sexual
    abstinence, 22, 25
    code of behavior, 28
    intercourse, 15, 18-19,
        22-23
    lifestyle, 19
    orientation, 12
sexually transmitted
  diseases (STDs),
        definition of, 9
signs, 25
sterility, 10
support groups, 42-43
sweat, 21
symptoms, 15, 25, 31-33
syphilis, 11, 14, 88
syringe, 19, 24

T
tattooing, 20
tears, 21
teenagers, 12-13, 22, 38
telephone numbers, 39, 43
testing, 39-40
trichomoniasis, 11, 89

U
urethritis, 10
urine, 21

V
vaccine, 10, 24
vagina, 19, 76-77
vaginal
   fluids, 18-19, 22
   intercourse, 18
venereal diseases (VD),
   definition of, 9
virus, 10, 15, 30

W
warts (see genital warts)
washing, 23

STD/HIV Summary Sheet

S exually transmitted diseases (STDs), including HIV infection and AIDS, are a major health problem. Over 40 million persons are affected each year in the United States. Most STD/HIV cases occur in persons in their mid teens through their 40s. In the United States, a teenager gets an STD every 13 seconds. Untreated STD/HIV can lead to sterility, pelvic inflammatory disease, infant damage, mental illness, and death. Anyone, regardless of sex, race, social status, or sexual orientation can get STD/HIV. What a person does — not who they are — exposes them to STD/HIV.

WHAT ARE STD/HIV? More than 25 diseases are classified as STDs. Important STDs include chlamydial infections, genital herpes, genital warts, gonorrhea, hepatitis, HIV infection and AIDS, pediculosis pubis, syphilis, and trichomoniasis.

HOW ARE STD/HIV SPREAD? STD/HIV are caused by germs passed during sexual contact, such as vaginal and anal intercourse, and oral sex. HIV, the virus that causes AIDS, can also be passed in blood from the sharing of injecting drug equipment. An infected mother can pass STD/HIV to her child. A person can get the same STD many times.

AVOIDING STD/HIV. Not having sexual intercourse (abstinence) is the surest way of not getting STD/HIV. Two uninfected people having sex only with each other is the next best method. Persons with many sex partners have the greatest chance of getting STD/HIV. People can reduce their chances of infection by using a latex condom and avoiding people who are at risk, such as those having many sex partners. Another way of avoiding STD/HIV is not to have sexual contact with injecting drug users or sharing injecting drug equipment. Persons with different partners, especially females, should have regular STD/HIV check-ups.

RECOGNIZING AN STD/HIV INFECTION. Persons having sex, especially those with different partners, need to be alert for STD/HIV symptoms. The major STD symptoms are: (1) genital discharge; (2) abdominal pain; (3) pain during urination; (4) skin changes; (5) genital itching; and (6) flu-like symptoms. The first symptoms of HIV infection include: (1) tiredness; (2) swollen lymph glands; (3) fever; (4) loss of appetite; (5) loss of weight; (6) diarrhea; and (7) night sweats. HIV symptoms can be similar to common minor illnesses. STD/HIV symptoms are sometimes hidden or unnoticed. Many females with an STD have no symptoms. For some STDs, the symptoms disappear without the disease being treated. But, most STDs can be passed to others when the symptoms are not present. Persons suspecting an STD/HIV infection should stop having sex, go to a doctor or clinic right away, and take their partners with them.

SEEKING TREATMENT. Persons who think they might have STD/HIV should not try to diagnose or treat their own condition. Only a doctor can do those things. Most STDs can be cured easily and quickly. HIV infection and AIDS and genital herpes cannot be cured. No damage may occur if an STD is treated soon enough. STD/HIV diagnosis and treatment are available from: (1) STD and HIV/AIDS clinics; (2) private doctors; (3) family planning clinics; and (4) hospitals. Calling the local health department is one of the best ways of finding STD/HIV medical care in your town. The health department is usually listed in the telephone book yellow pages under county or city government offices. Sometimes the health department is listed in the white pages under "health," or in the blue pages of government listings. To get the location of the nearest STD or HIV/AIDS clinic or to get the latest information, call (for free) the National STD Hotline (1-800-227-8922) or the National AIDS Hotline (1-800-342-AIDS). Spanish speaking callers, dial 1-800-344-SIDA and hearing impaired callers, dial 1-800-AIDS TTY. In every state, minors can get STD/HIV counseling, testing, and treatment without parental consent. Anyone being treated for STD/HIV should follow the doctor's directions.

GETTING PARTNERS TO TREATMENT. Persons with STD/HIV should be sure to get their partners to medical care. This is best done by taking the partner to a doctor or health clinic. The partner can be told in person or over the phone that he or she might be infected. A person can ask the doctor to have the partner informed by an STD/HIV public health specialist.

CONCLUSION. Each person's effort is the best way of stopping STD/HIV. People do this by being responsible for personal health and the health of any sex partners. A person can help wipe out STD/HIV myths by being a source of accurate STD/HIV facts and by being helpful and supportive of friends who get an STD/HIV. Also, a person can serve as a responsible role model and promote healthy peer norms.

About the Author

Dr. William L. Yarber is a professor of health education in the Department of Applied Health Science at Indiana University, Bloomington. He is a former public school health science and biology teacher. Yarber was named the 1991 Scholar of the Association for the Advancement of Health Education, and received the 1991 President's Award for Distinguished Teaching at Indiana University. Yarber chaired a task force of leading sexuality educators that published the first national consensus guidelines for comprehensive sexuality education, K-12. He also has taught at Purdue University and the University of Minnesota.

Professor Yarber has published extensively in scholarly journals in the areas of HIV and sexually transmitted diseases education, and sexuality education. He published the school curricula, *Looking into AIDS, AIDS: What Young People Should Know*, and *STD: A Guide for Today's Young Adults*.

Dr. Yarber has served as consultant on school AIDS and STD education for the World Health Organization Global Program on AIDS, UNESCO, and the U.S. Public Health Service's Centers for Disease Control. He has presented papers at numerous national and international conferences and has conducted workshops on AIDS and STD education for school districts and professional organizations in the United States and other countries.

This curriculum is dedicated to Margaret, Brooke, Jessica, Bill, and Beulah.